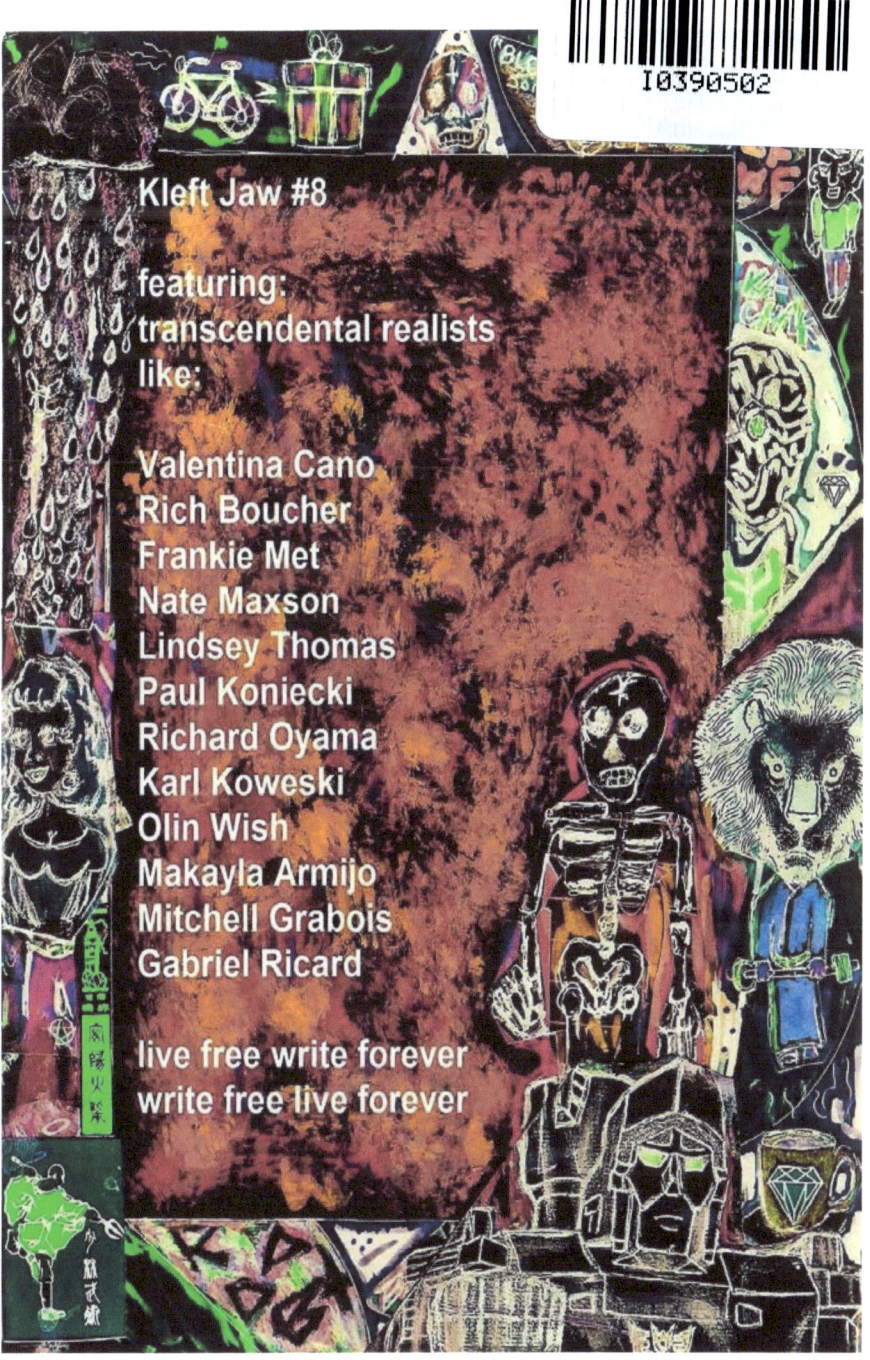

Kleft Jaw #8

featuring:
transcendental realists
like:

Valentina Cano
Rich Boucher
Frankie Met
Nate Maxson
Lindsey Thomas
Paul Koniecki
Richard Oyama
Karl Koweski
Olin Wish
Makayla Armijo
Mitchell Grabois
Gabriel Ricard

live free write forever
write free live forever

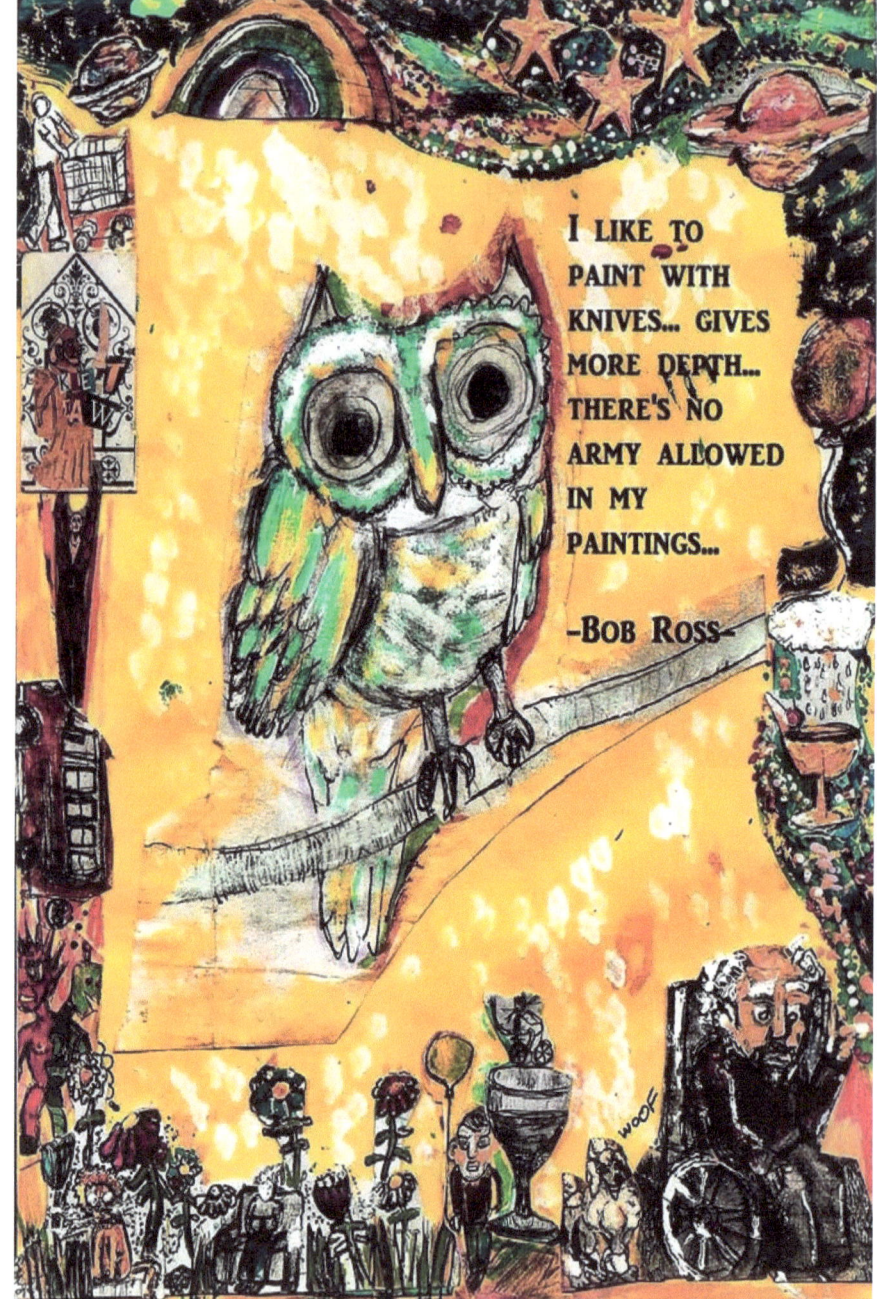

I LIKE TO PAINT WITH KNIVES... GIVES MORE DEPTH... THERE'S NO ARMY ALLOWED IN MY PAINTINGS...

-BOB ROSS-

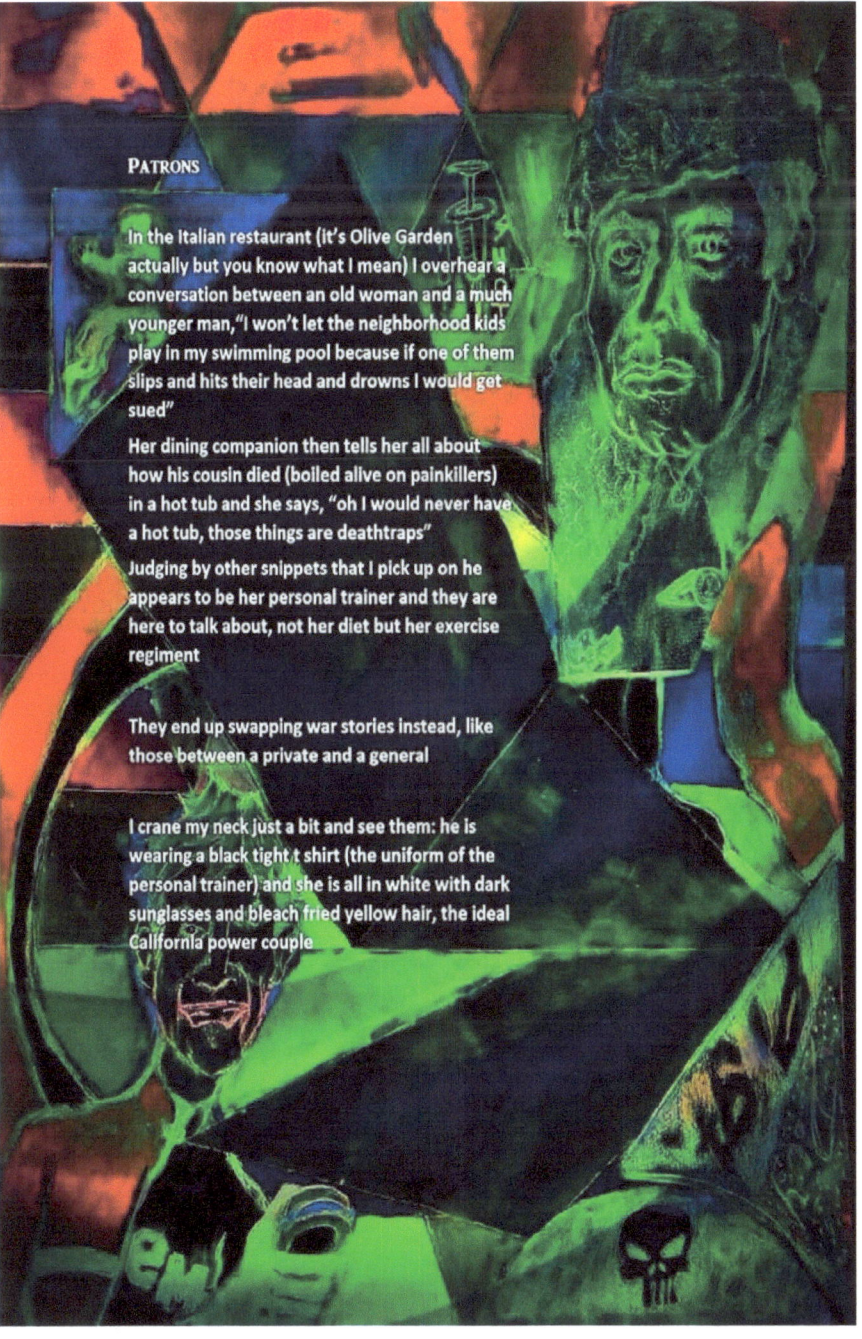

PATRONS

In the Italian restaurant (it's Olive Garden actually but you know what I mean) I overhear a conversation between an old woman and a much younger man, "I won't let the neighborhood kids play in my swimming pool because if one of them slips and hits their head and drowns I would get sued"

Her dining companion then tells her all about how his cousin died (boiled alive on painkillers) in a hot tub and she says, "oh I would never have a hot tub, those things are deathtraps"

Judging by other snippets that I pick up on he appears to be her personal trainer and they are here to talk about, not her diet but her exercise regiment

They end up swapping war stories instead, like those between a private and a general

I crane my neck just a bit and see them: he is wearing a black tight t shirt (the uniform of the personal trainer) and she is all in white with dark sunglasses and bleach fried yellow hair, the ideal California power couple

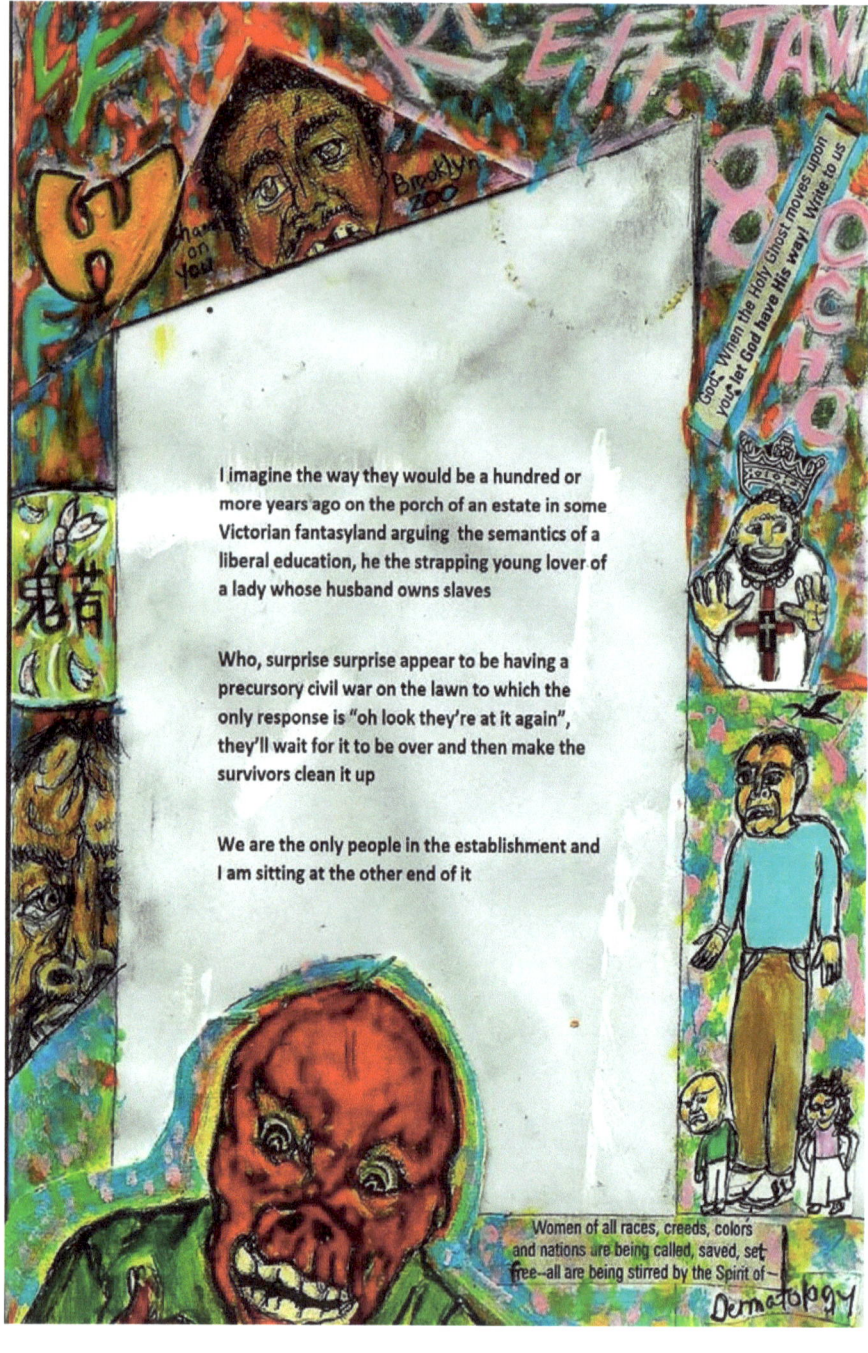

I imagine the way they would be a hundred or more years ago on the porch of an estate in some Victorian fantasyland arguing the semantics of a liberal education, he the strapping young lover of a lady whose husband owns slaves

Who, surprise surprise appear to be having a precursory civil war on the lawn to which the only response is "oh look they're at it again", they'll wait for it to be over and then make the survivors clean it up

We are the only people in the establishment and I am sitting at the other end of it

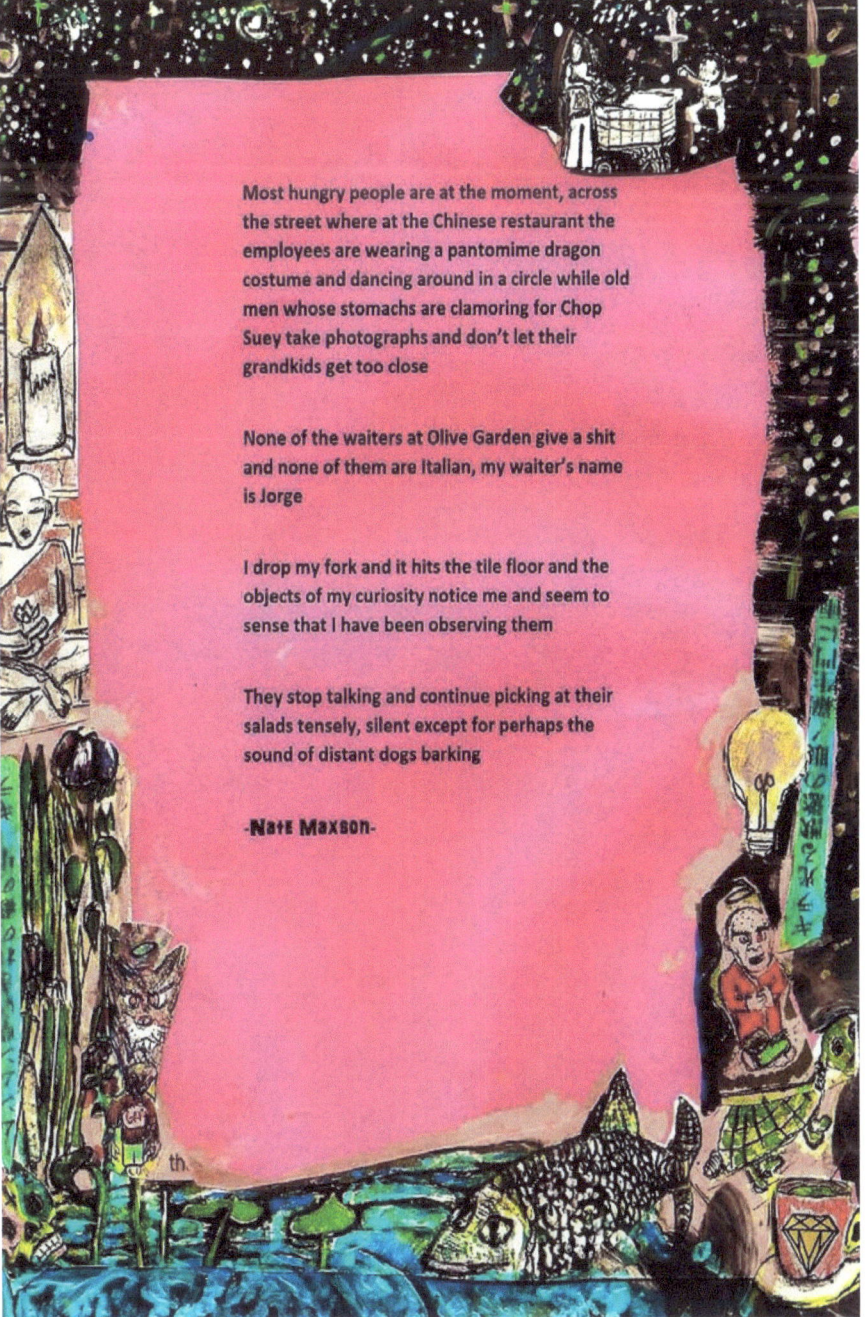

Most hungry people are at the moment, across the street where at the Chinese restaurant the employees are wearing a pantomime dragon costume and dancing around in a circle while old men whose stomachs are clamoring for Chop Suey take photographs and don't let their grandkids get too close

None of the waiters at Olive Garden give a shit and none of them are Italian, my waiter's name is Jorge

I drop my fork and it hits the tile floor and the objects of my curiosity notice me and seem to sense that I have been observing them

They stop talking and continue picking at their salads tensely, silent except for perhaps the sound of distant dogs barking

-Nate Maxson-

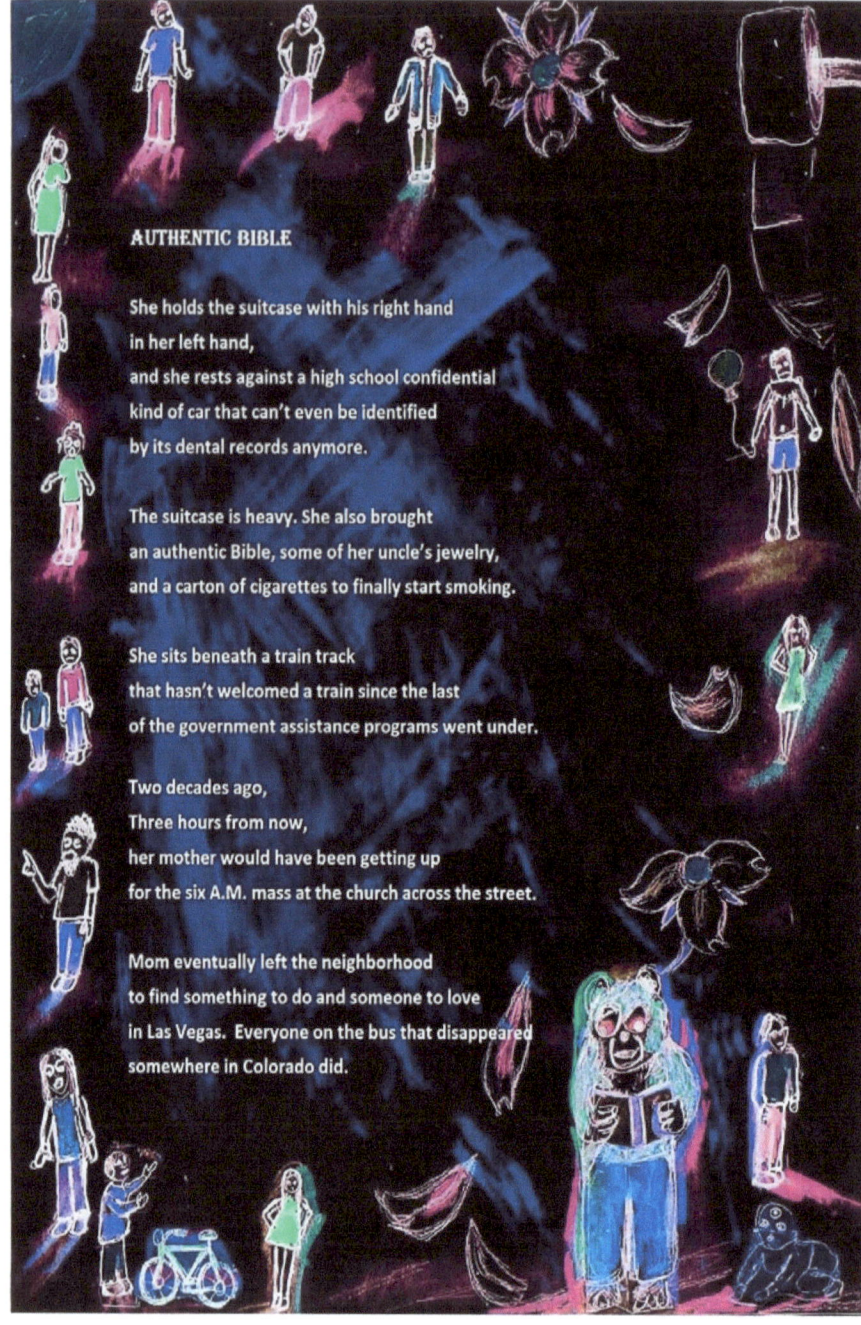

AUTHENTIC BIBLE

She holds the suitcase with his right hand
in her left hand,
and she rests against a high school confidential
kind of car that can't even be identified
by its dental records anymore.

The suitcase is heavy. She also brought
an authentic Bible, some of her uncle's jewelry,
and a carton of cigarettes to finally start smoking.

She sits beneath a train track
that hasn't welcomed a train since the last
of the government assistance programs went under.

Two decades ago,
Three hours from now,
her mother would have been getting up
for the six A.M. mass at the church across the street.

Mom eventually left the neighborhood
to find something to do and someone to love
in Las Vegas. Everyone on the bus that disappeared
somewhere in Colorado did.

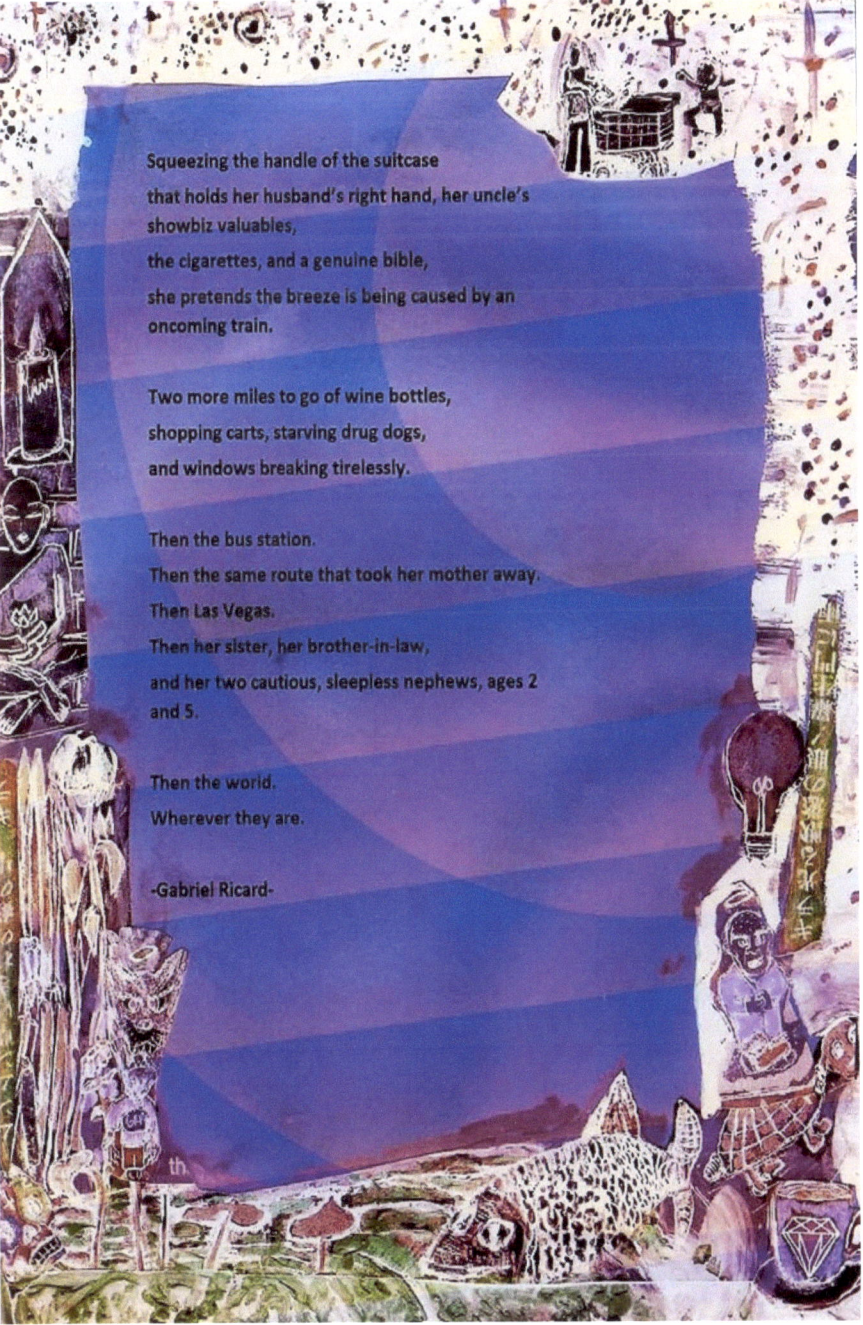

Squeezing the handle of the suitcase
that holds her husband's right hand, her uncle's
showbiz valuables,
the cigarettes, and a genuine bible,
she pretends the breeze is being caused by an
oncoming train.

Two more miles to go of wine bottles,
shopping carts, starving drug dogs,
and windows breaking tirelessly.

Then the bus station.
Then the same route that took her mother away.
Then Las Vegas.
Then her sister, her brother-in-law,
and her two cautious, sleepless nephews, ages 2
and 5.

Then the world.
Wherever they are.

-Gabriel Ricard-

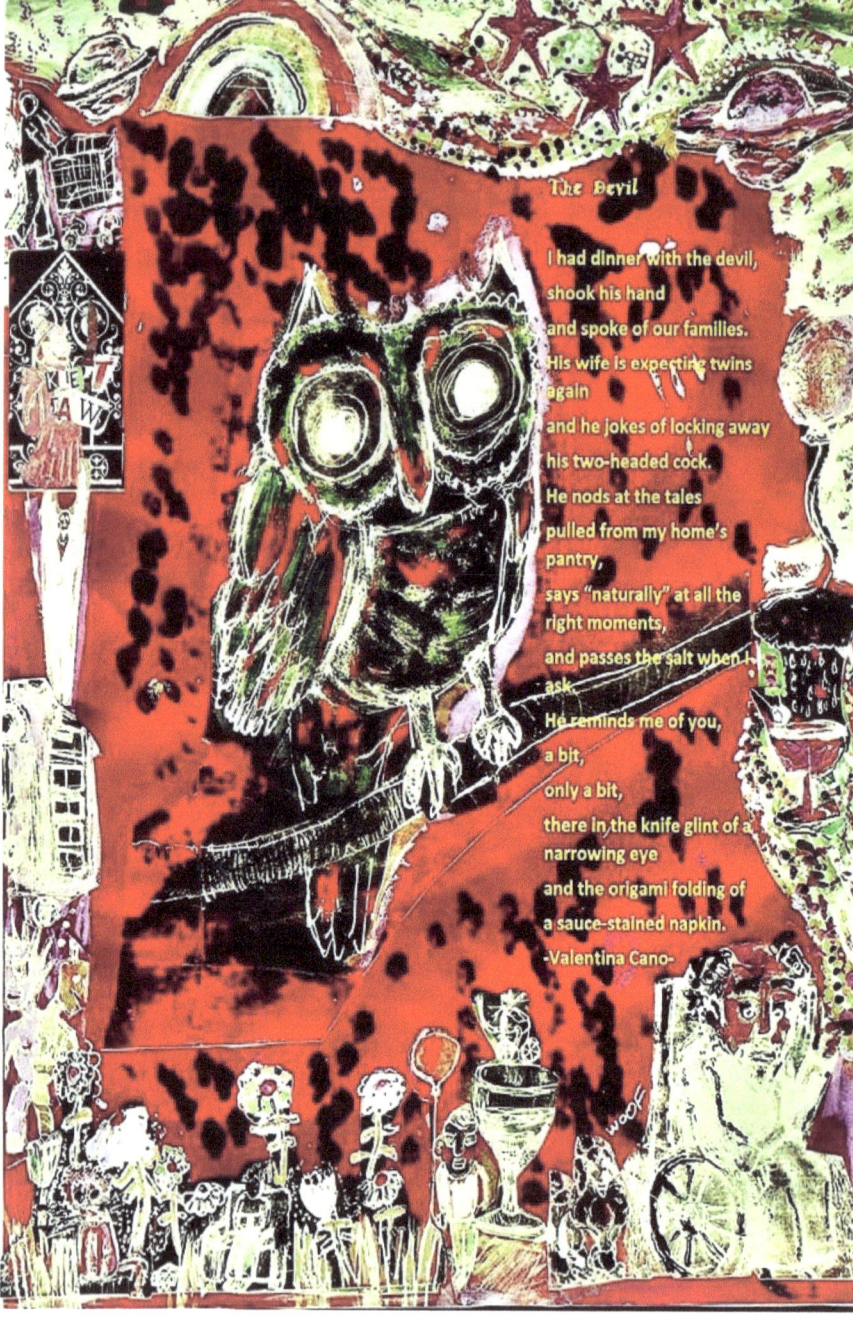

The Devil

I had dinner with the devil,
shook his hand
and spoke of our families.
His wife is expecting twins
again
and he jokes of locking away
his two-headed cock.
He nods at the tales
pulled from my home's
pantry,
says "naturally" at all the
right moments,
and passes the salt when I
ask.
He reminds me of you,
a bit,
only a bit,
there in the knife glint of a
narrowing eye
and the origami folding of
a sauce-stained napkin.
-Valentina Cano-

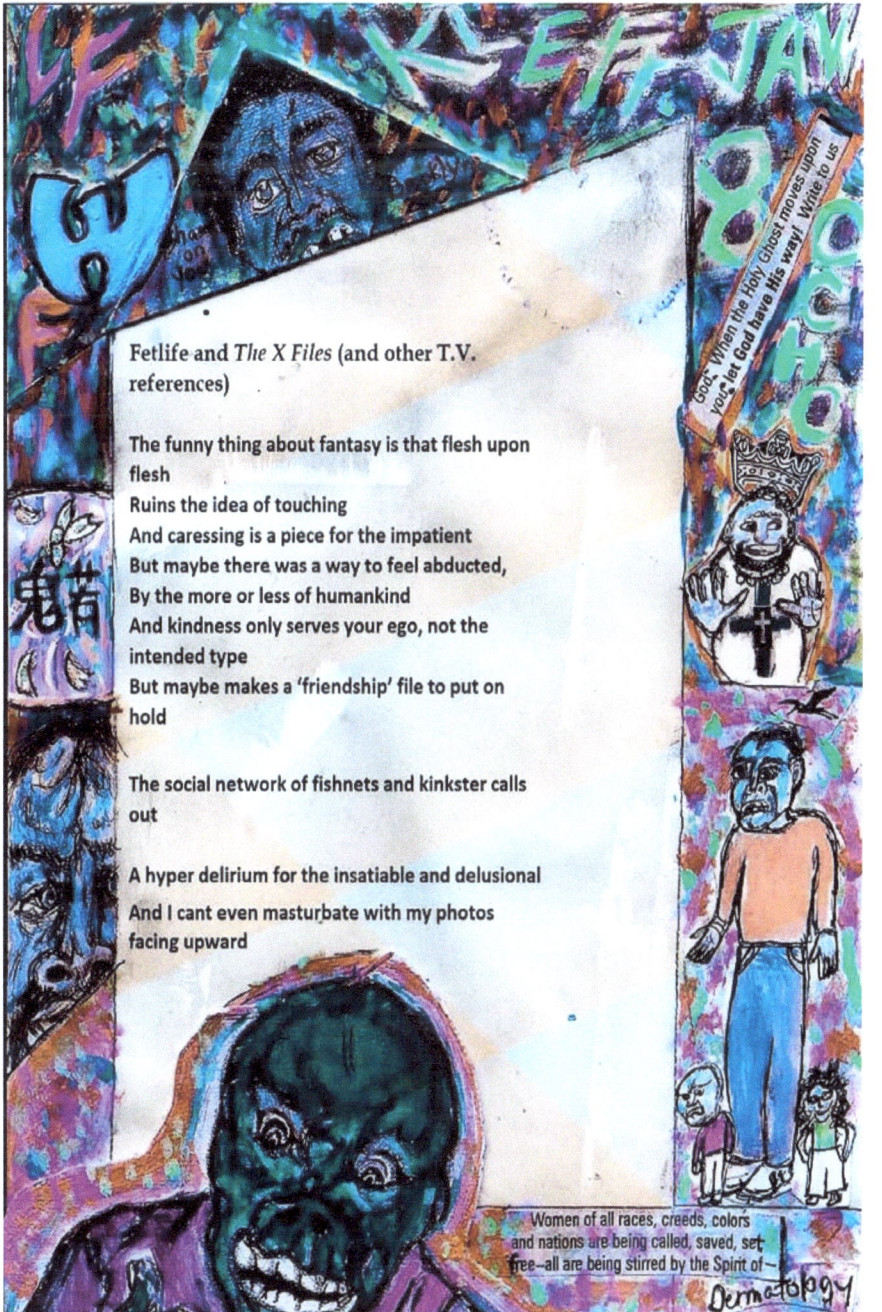

Fetlife and *The X Files* (and other T.V. references)

The funny thing about fantasy is that flesh upon flesh
Ruins the idea of touching
And caressing is a piece for the impatient
But maybe there was a way to feel abducted,
By the more or less of humankind
And kindness only serves your ego, not the intended type
But maybe makes a 'friendship' file to put on hold

The social network of fishnets and kinkster calls out

A hyper delirium for the insatiable and delusional
And I cant even masturbate with my photos facing upward

Dermatology

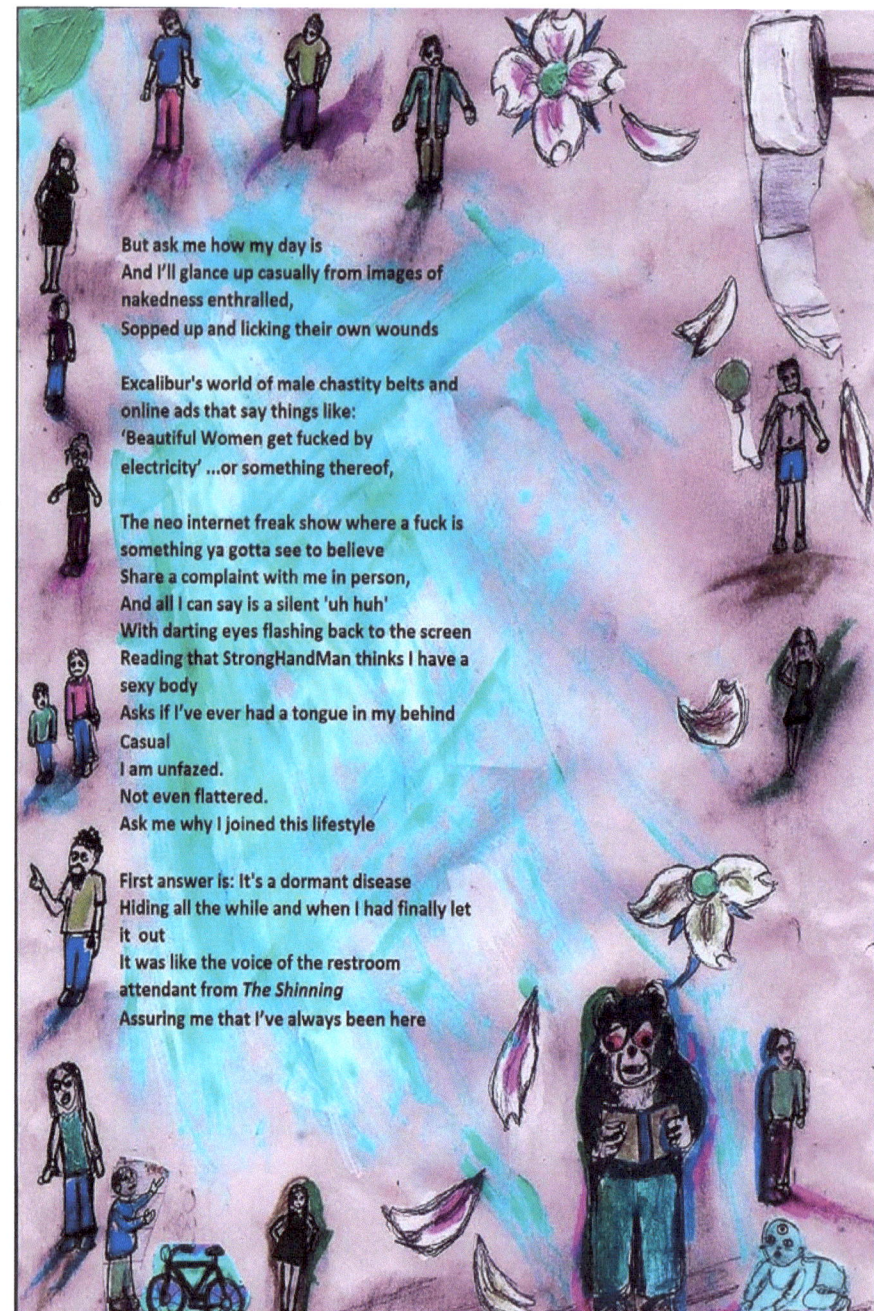

But ask me how my day is
And I'll glance up casually from images of
nakedness enthralled,
Sopped up and licking their own wounds

Excalibur's world of male chastity belts and
online ads that say things like:
'Beautiful Women get fucked by
electricity' ...or something thereof,

The neo internet freak show where a fuck is
something ya gotta see to believe
Share a complaint with me in person,
And all I can say is a silent 'uh huh'
With darting eyes flashing back to the screen
Reading that StrongHandMan thinks I have a
sexy body
Asks if I've ever had a tongue in my behind
Casual
I am unfazed.
Not even flattered.
Ask me why I joined this lifestyle

First answer is: It's a dormant disease
Hiding all the while and when I had finally let
it out
It was like the voice of the restroom
attendant from *The Shinning*
Assuring me that I've always been here

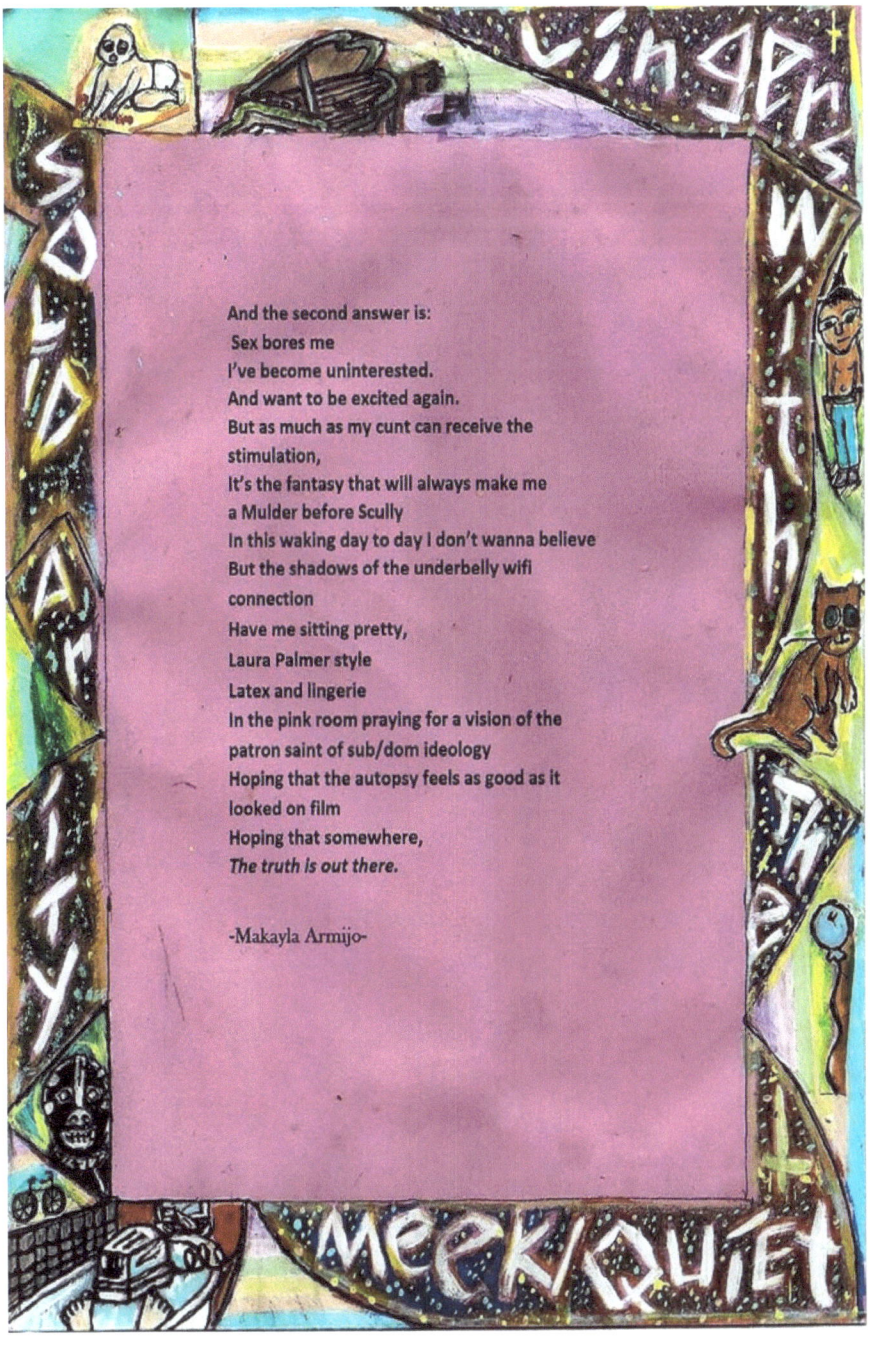

And the second answer is:
Sex bores me
I've become uninterested.
And want to be excited again.
But as much as my cunt can receive the
stimulation,
It's the fantasy that will always make me
a Mulder before Scully
In this waking day to day I don't wanna believe
But the shadows of the underbelly wifi
connection
Have me sitting pretty,
Laura Palmer style
Latex and lingerie
In the pink room praying for a vision of the
patron saint of sub/dom ideology
Hoping that the autopsy feels as good as it
looked on film
Hoping that somewhere,
The truth is out there.

-Makayla Armijo-

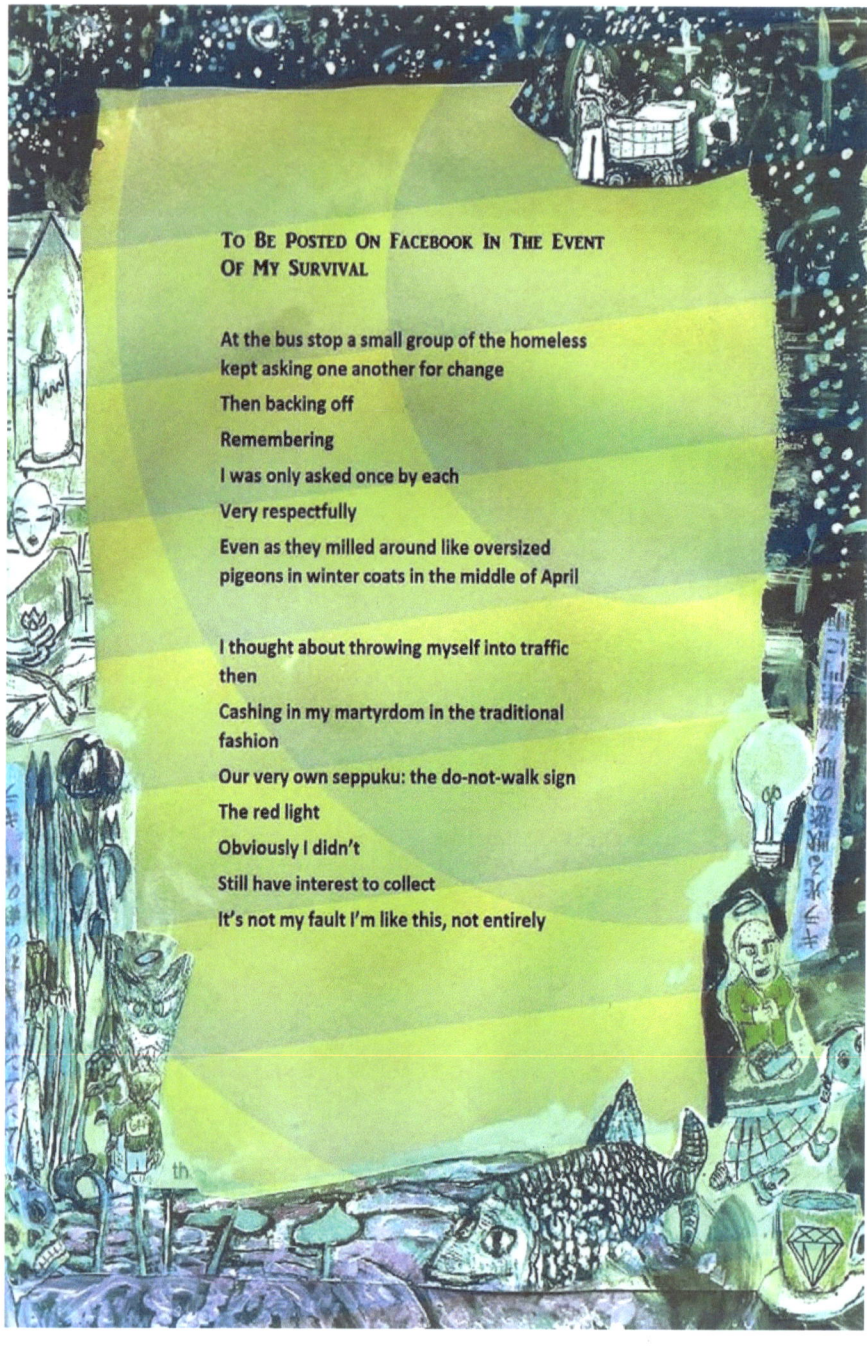

TO BE POSTED ON FACEBOOK IN THE EVENT OF MY SURVIVAL

At the bus stop a small group of the homeless
kept asking one another for change

Then backing off

Remembering

I was only asked once by each

Very respectfully

Even as they milled around like oversized
pigeons in winter coats in the middle of April

I thought about throwing myself into traffic
then

Cashing in my martyrdom in the traditional
fashion

Our very own seppuku: the do-not-walk sign

The red light

Obviously I didn't

Still have interest to collect

It's not my fault I'm like this, not entirely

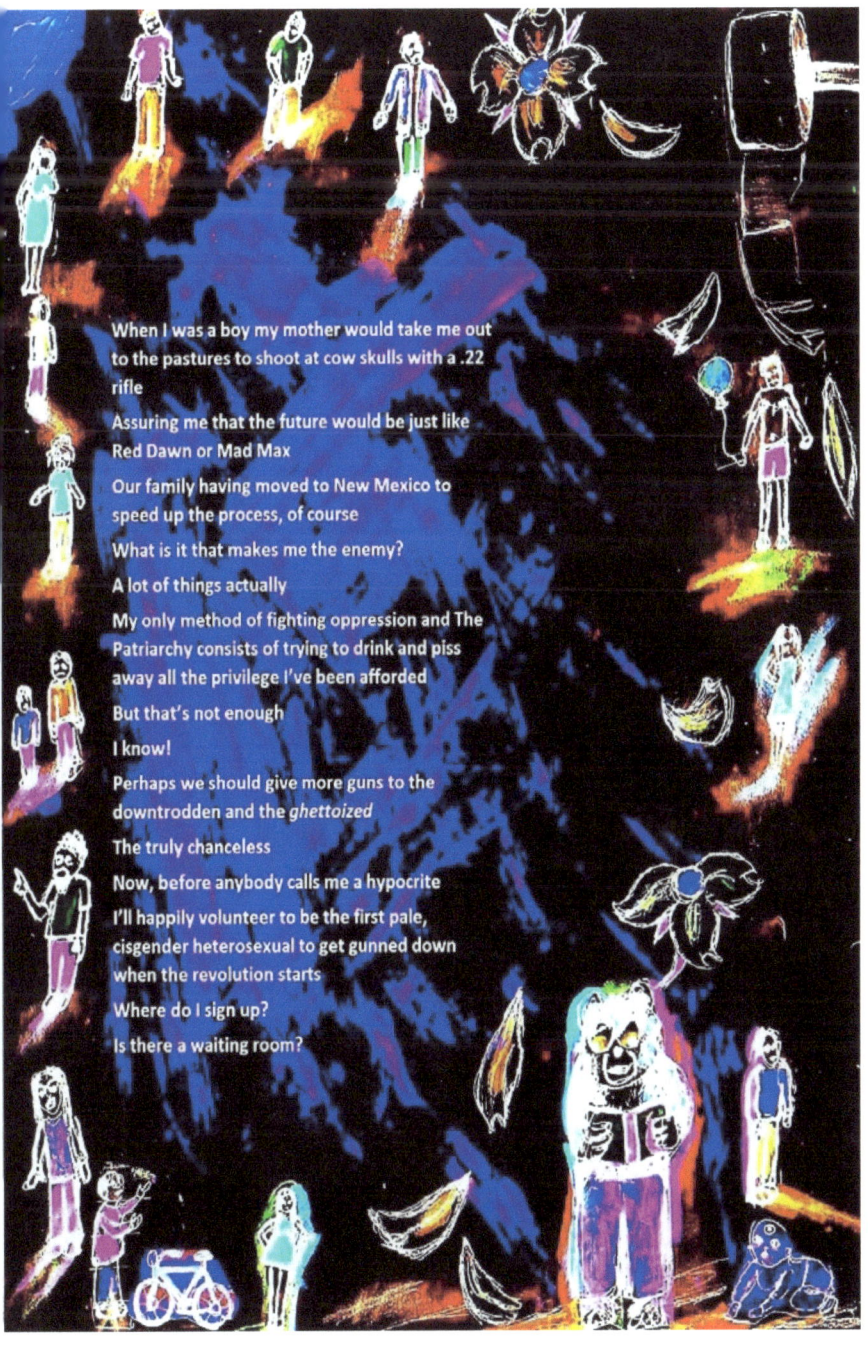

When I was a boy my mother would take me out to the pastures to shoot at cow skulls with a .22 rifle

Assuring me that the future would be just like Red Dawn or Mad Max

Our family having moved to New Mexico to speed up the process, of course

What is it that makes me the enemy?

A lot of things actually

My only method of fighting oppression and The Patriarchy consists of trying to drink and piss away all the privilege I've been afforded

But that's not enough

I know!

Perhaps we should give more guns to the downtrodden and the *ghettoized*

The truly chanceless

Now, before anybody calls me a hypocrite

I'll happily volunteer to be the first pale, cisgender heterosexual to get gunned down when the revolution starts

Where do I sign up?

Is there a waiting room?

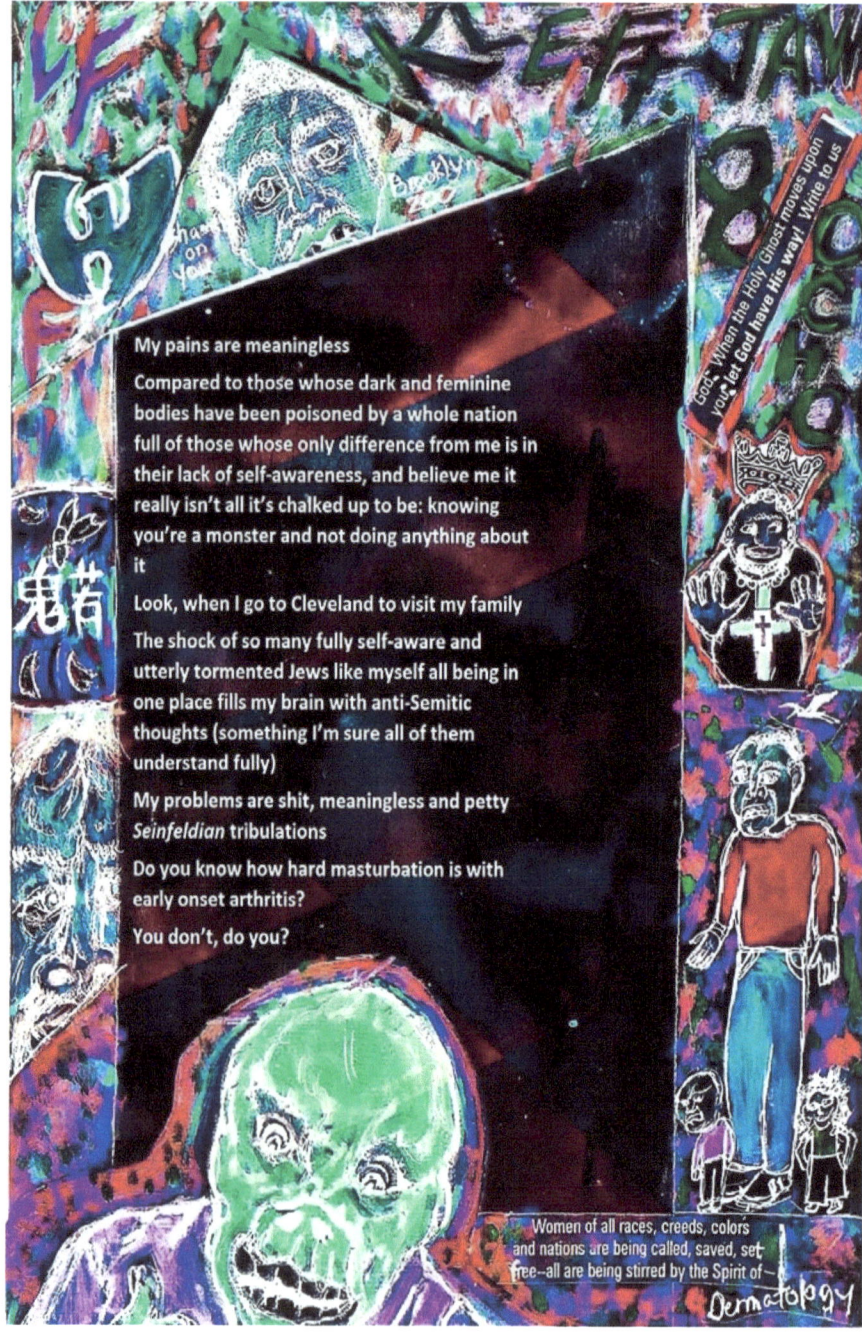

My pains are meaningless

Compared to those whose dark and feminine bodies have been poisoned by a whole nation full of those whose only difference from me is in their lack of self-awareness, and believe me it really isn't all it's chalked up to be: knowing you're a monster and not doing anything about it

Look, when I go to Cleveland to visit my family

The shock of so many fully self-aware and utterly tormented Jews like myself all being in one place fills my brain with anti-Semitic thoughts (something I'm sure all of them understand fully)

My problems are shit, meaningless and petty *Seinfeldian* tribulations

Do you know how hard masturbation is with early onset arthritis?

You don't, do you?

God: When the Holy Ghost moves upon your, let God have His way! Write to us

Women of all races, creeds, colors and nations are being called, saved, set free--all are being stirred by the Spirit of ~

Dermatology

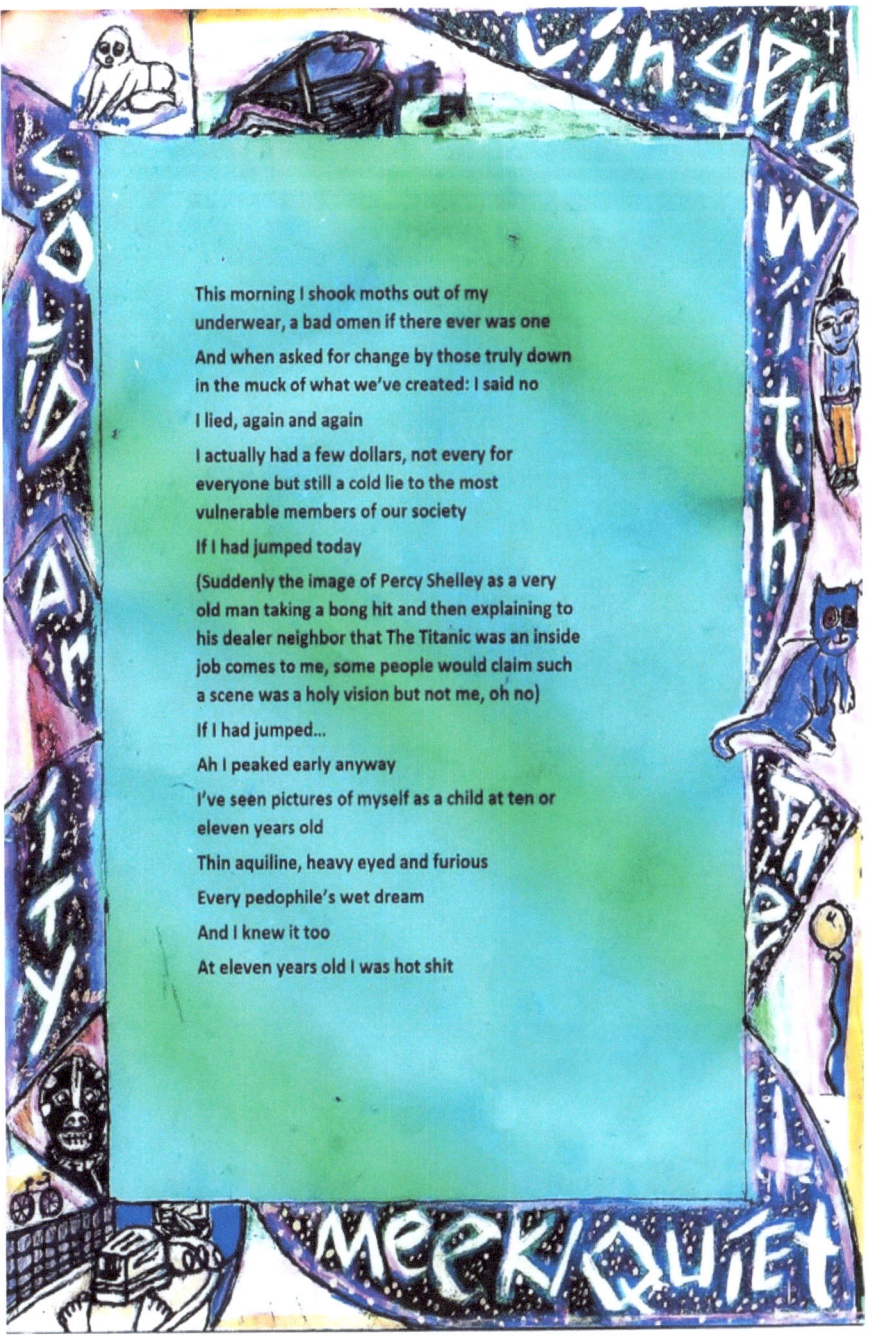

This morning I shook moths out of my
underwear, a bad omen if there ever was one

And when asked for change by those truly down
in the muck of what we've created: I said no

I lied, again and again

I actually had a few dollars, not every for
everyone but still a cold lie to the most
vulnerable members of our society

If I had jumped today

(Suddenly the image of Percy Shelley as a very
old man taking a bong hit and then explaining to
his dealer neighbor that The Titanic was an inside
job comes to me, some people would claim such
a scene was a holy vision but not me, oh no)

If I had jumped...

Ah I peaked early anyway

I've seen pictures of myself as a child at ten or
eleven years old

Thin aquiline, heavy eyed and furious

Every pedophile's wet dream

And I knew it too

At eleven years old I was hot shit

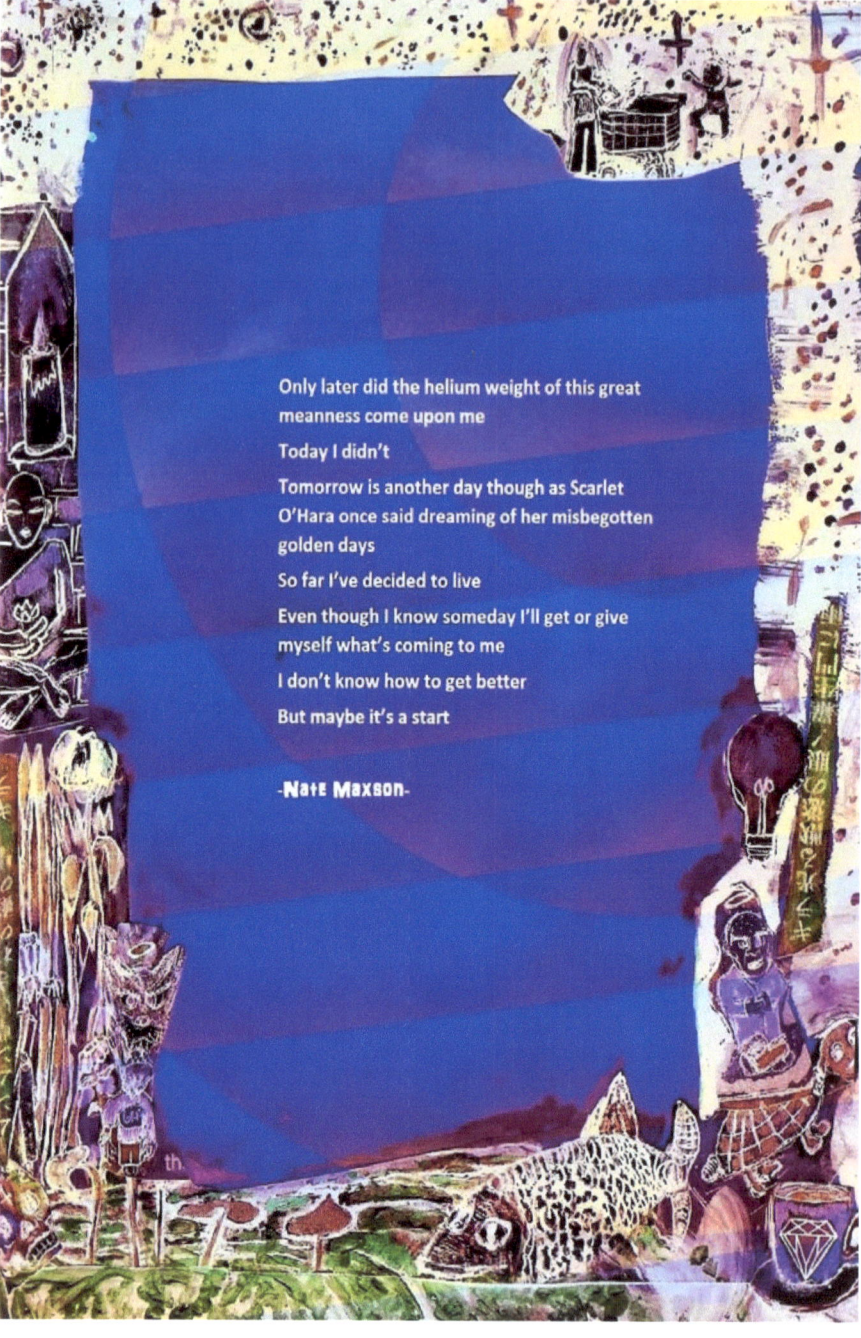

Only later did the helium weight of this great meanness come upon me

Today I didn't

Tomorrow is another day though as Scarlet O'Hara once said dreaming of her misbegotten golden days

So far I've decided to live

Even though I know someday I'll get or give myself what's coming to me

I don't know how to get better

But maybe it's a start

-Nate Maxson-

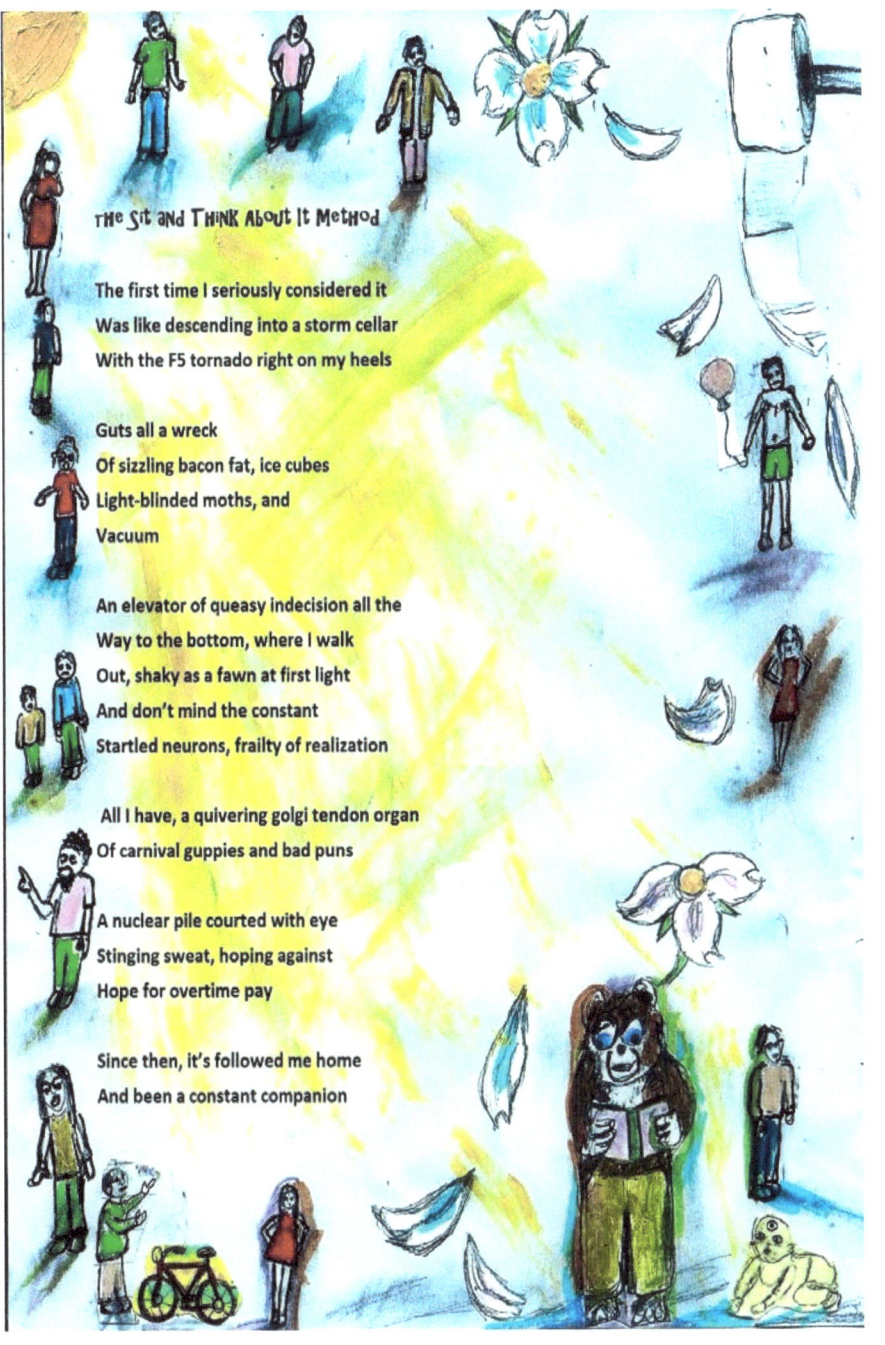

The Sit and Think About It Method

The first time I seriously considered it
Was like descending into a storm cellar
With the F5 tornado right on my heels

Guts all a wreck
Of sizzling bacon fat, ice cubes
Light-blinded moths, and
Vacuum

An elevator of queasy indecision all the
Way to the bottom, where I walk
Out, shaky as a fawn at first light
And don't mind the constant
Startled neurons, frailty of realization

All I have, a quivering golgi tendon organ
Of carnival guppies and bad puns

A nuclear pile courted with eye
Stinging sweat, hoping against
Hope for overtime pay

Since then, it's followed me home
And been a constant companion

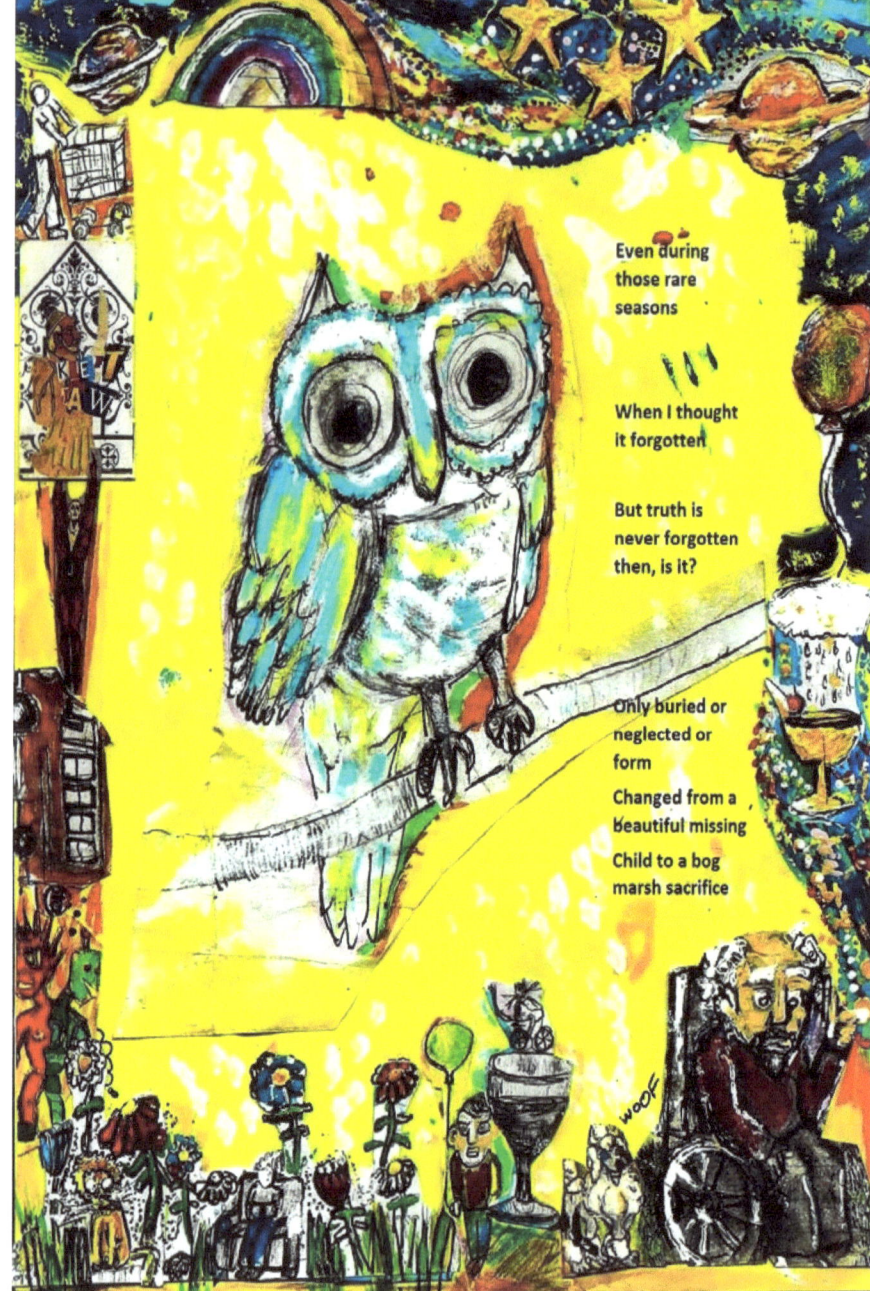

Even during
those rare
seasons

When I thought
it forgotten

But truth is
never forgotten
then, is it?

Only buried or
neglected or
form
Changed from a
beautiful missing
Child to a bog
marsh sacrifice

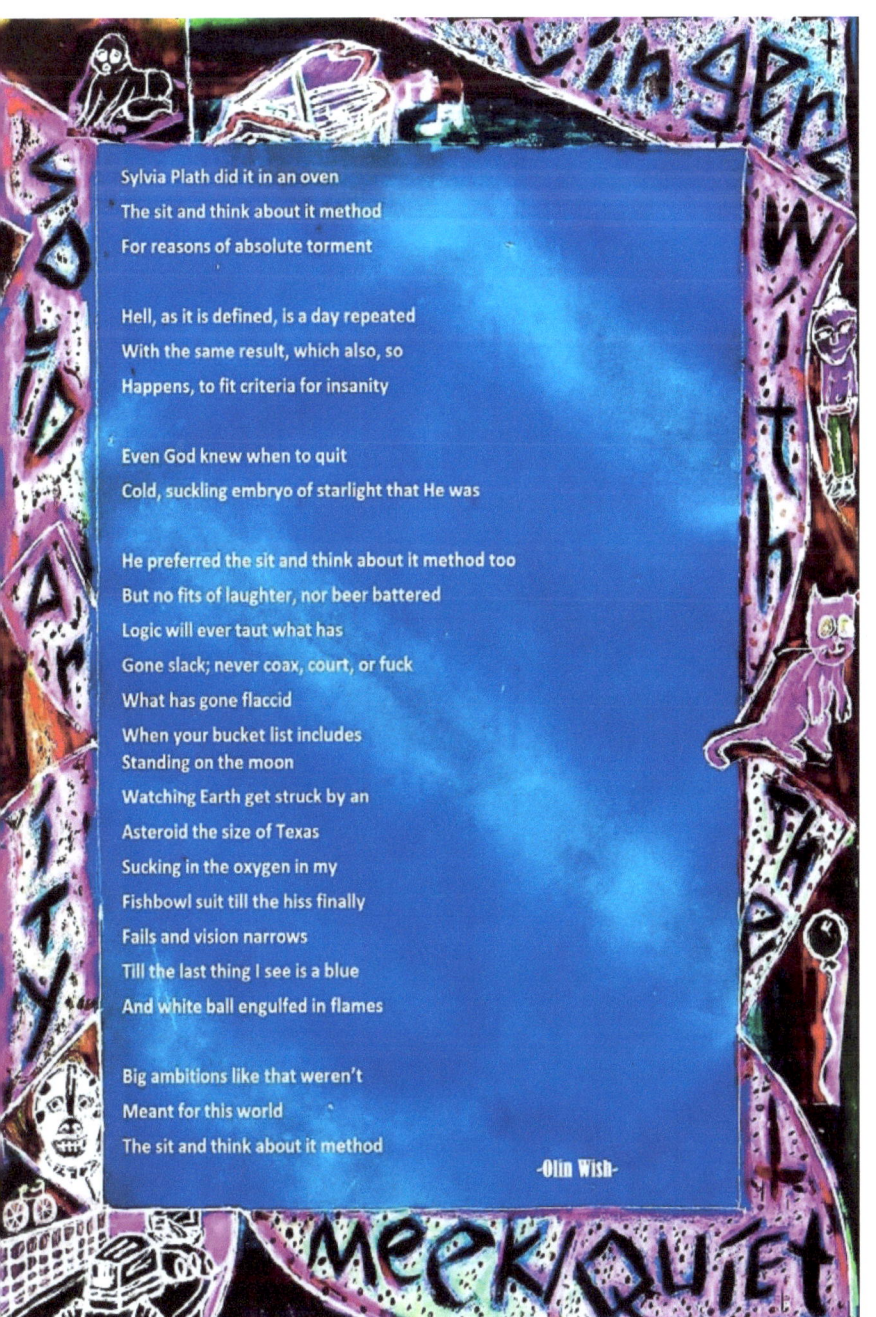

Sylvia Plath did it in an oven
The sit and think about it method
For reasons of absolute torment

Hell, as it is defined, is a day repeated
With the same result, which also, so
Happens, to fit criteria for insanity

Even God knew when to quit
Cold, suckling embryo of starlight that He was

He preferred the sit and think about it method too
But no fits of laughter, nor beer battered
Logic will ever taut what has
Gone slack; never coax, court, or fuck
What has gone flaccid
When your bucket list includes
Standing on the moon
Watching Earth get struck by an
Asteroid the size of Texas
Sucking in the oxygen in my
Fishbowl suit till the hiss finally
Fails and vision narrows
Till the last thing I see is a blue
And white ball engulfed in flames

Big ambitions like that weren't
Meant for this world
The sit and think about it method

-Olin Wish-

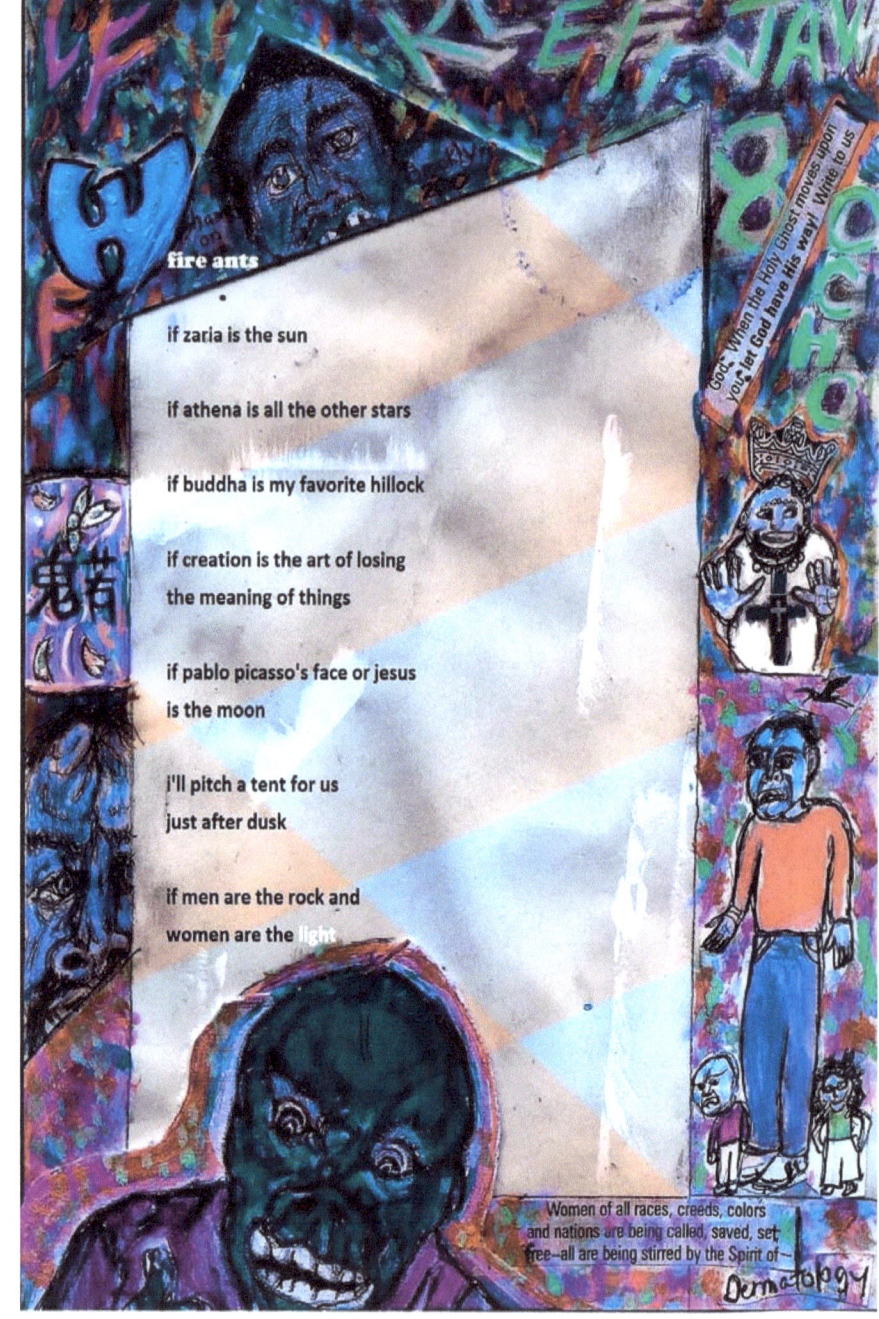

fire ants

if zaria is the sun

if athena is all the other stars

if buddha is my favorite hillock

if creation is the art of losing
the meaning of things

if pablo picasso's face or jesus
is the moon

i'll pitch a tent for us
just after dusk

if men are the rock and
women are the light

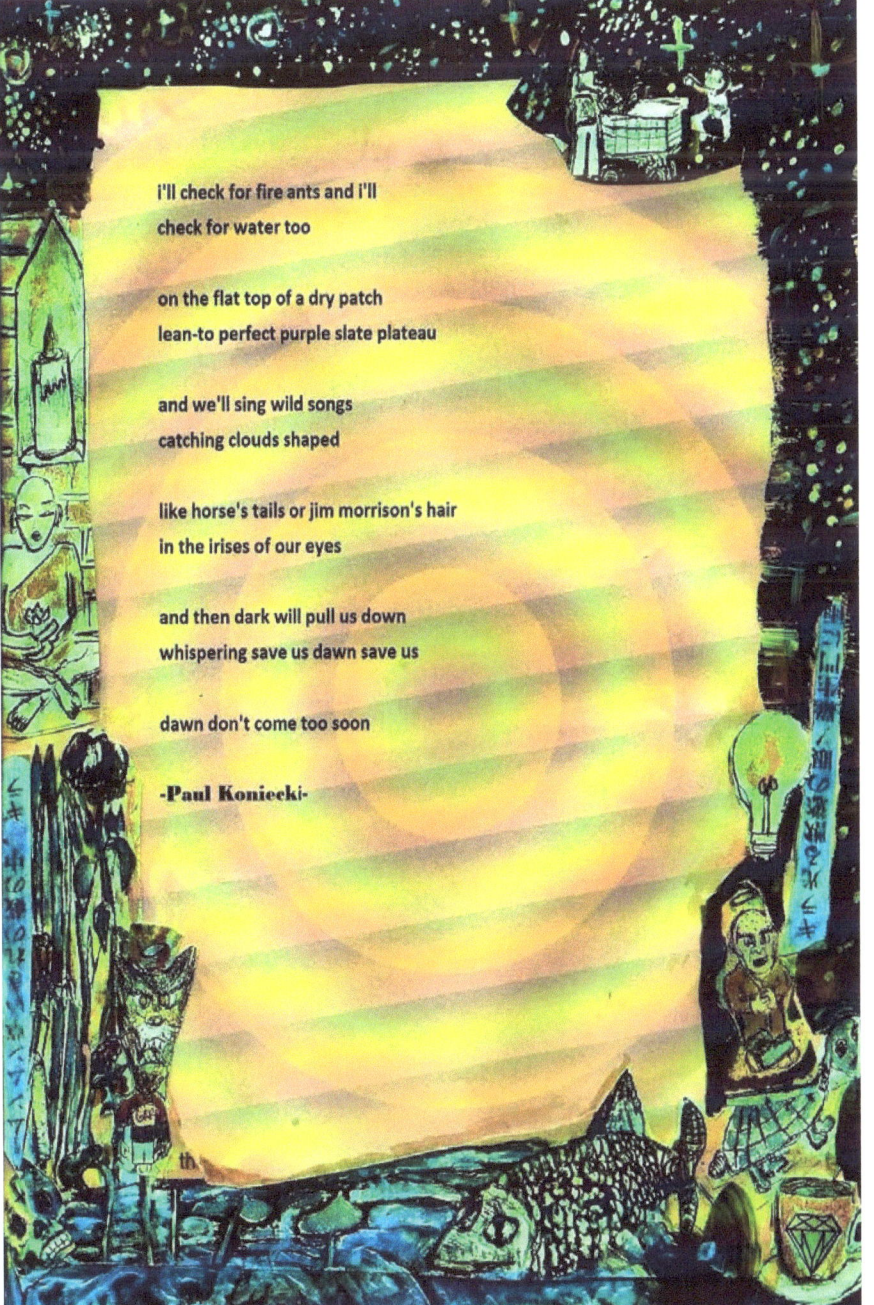

i'll check for fire ants and i'll
check for water too

on the flat top of a dry patch
lean-to perfect purple slate plateau

and we'll sing wild songs
catching clouds shaped

like horse's tails or jim morrison's hair
in the irises of our eyes

and then dark will pull us down
whispering save us dawn save us

dawn don't come too soon

-Paul Koniecki-

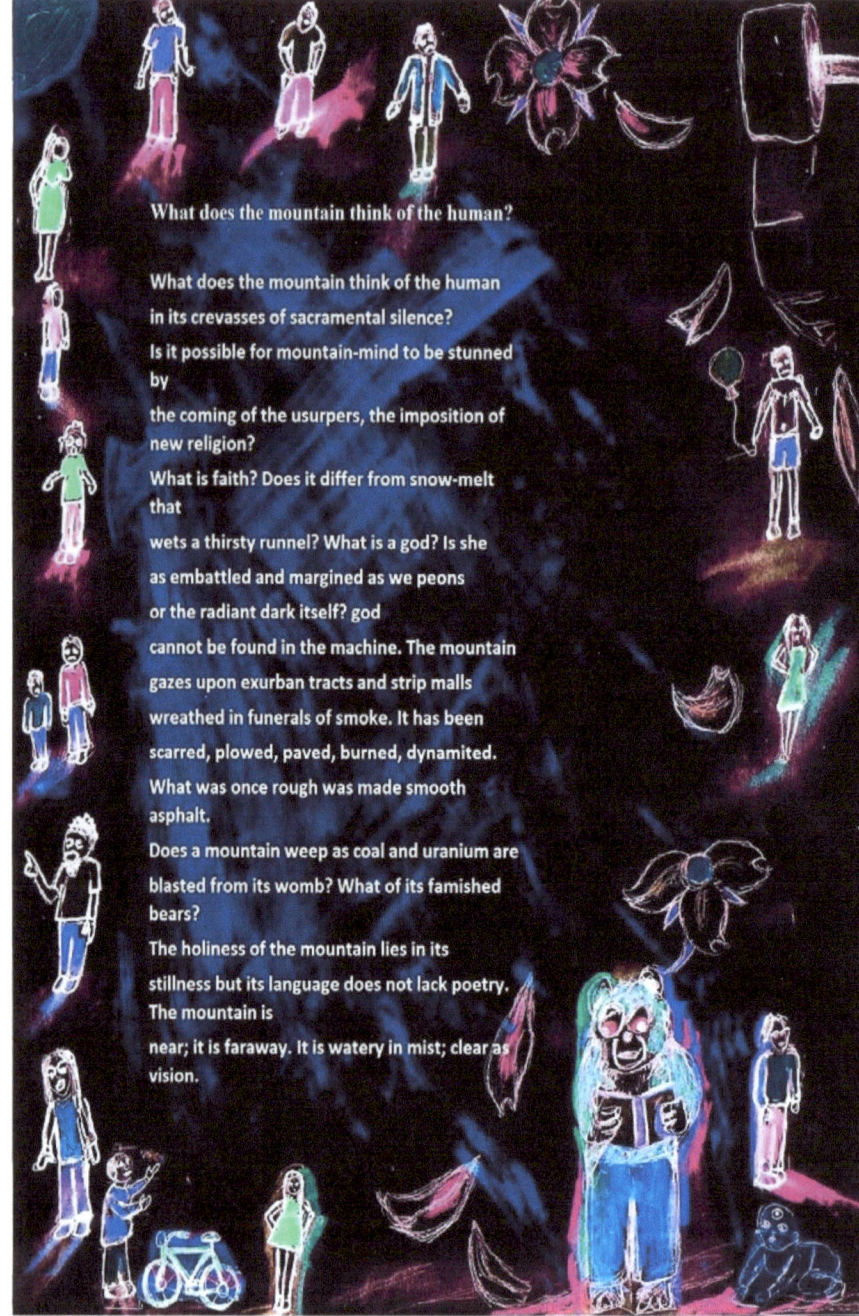

What does the mountain think of the human?

What does the mountain think of the human
in its crevasses of sacramental silence?
Is it possible for mountain-mind to be stunned
by
the coming of the usurpers, the imposition of
new religion?
What is faith? Does it differ from snow-melt
that
wets a thirsty runnel? What is a god? Is she
as embattled and margined as we peons
or the radiant dark itself? god
cannot be found in the machine. The mountain
gazes upon exurban tracts and strip malls
wreathed in funerals of smoke. It has been
scarred, plowed, paved, burned, dynamited.
What was once rough was made smooth
asphalt.
Does a mountain weep as coal and uranium are
blasted from its womb? What of its famished
bears?
The holiness of the mountain lies in its
stillness but its language does not lack poetry.
The mountain is
near; it is faraway. It is watery in mist; clear as
vision.

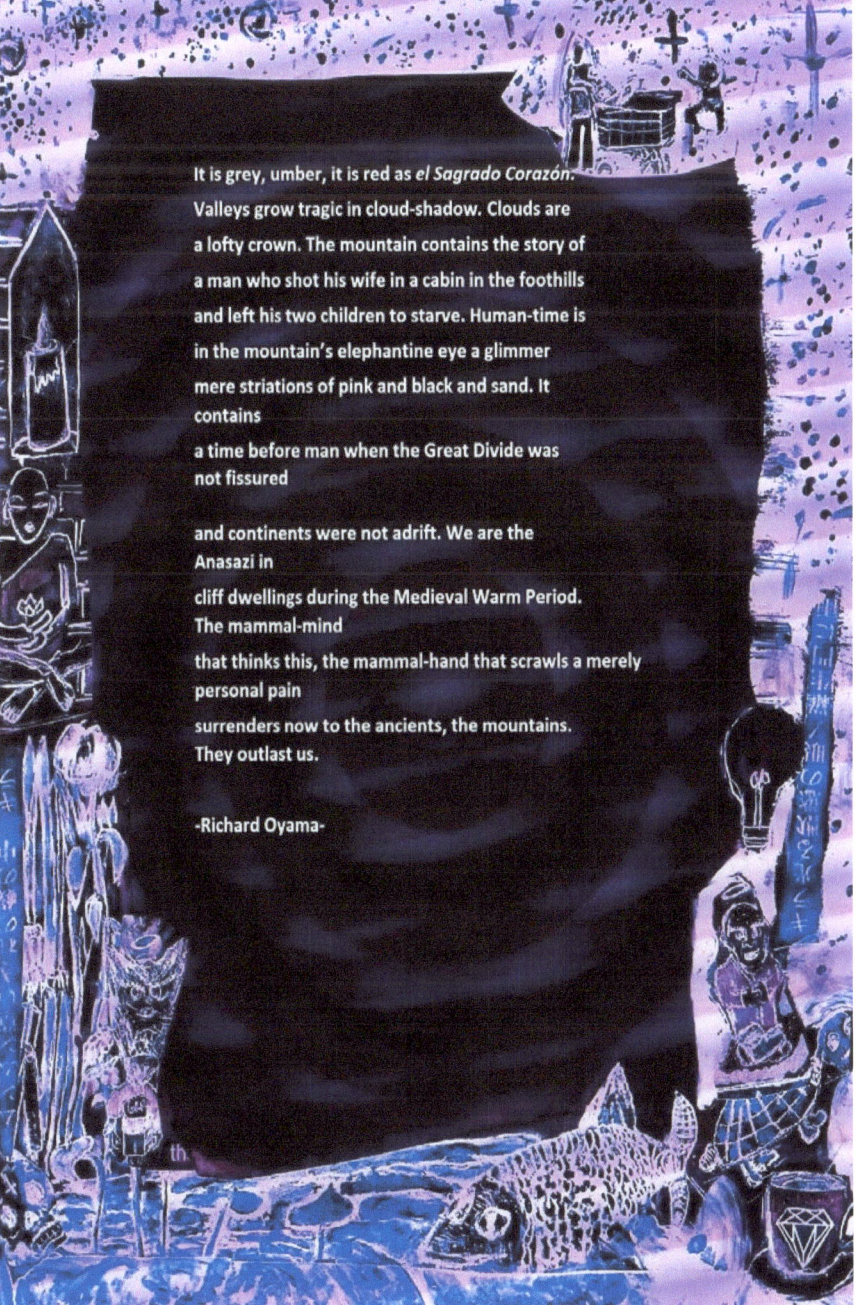

It is grey, umber, it is red as *el Sagrado Corazón*.

Valleys grow tragic in cloud-shadow. Clouds are

a lofty crown. The mountain contains the story of

a man who shot his wife in a cabin in the foothills

and left his two children to starve. Human-time is

in the mountain's elephantine eye a glimmer

mere striations of pink and black and sand. It contains

a time before man when the Great Divide was not fissured

and continents were not adrift. We are the Anasazi in

cliff dwellings during the Medieval Warm Period. The mammal-mind

that thinks this, the mammal-hand that scrawls a merely personal pain

surrenders now to the ancients, the mountains. They outlast us.

-Richard Oyama-

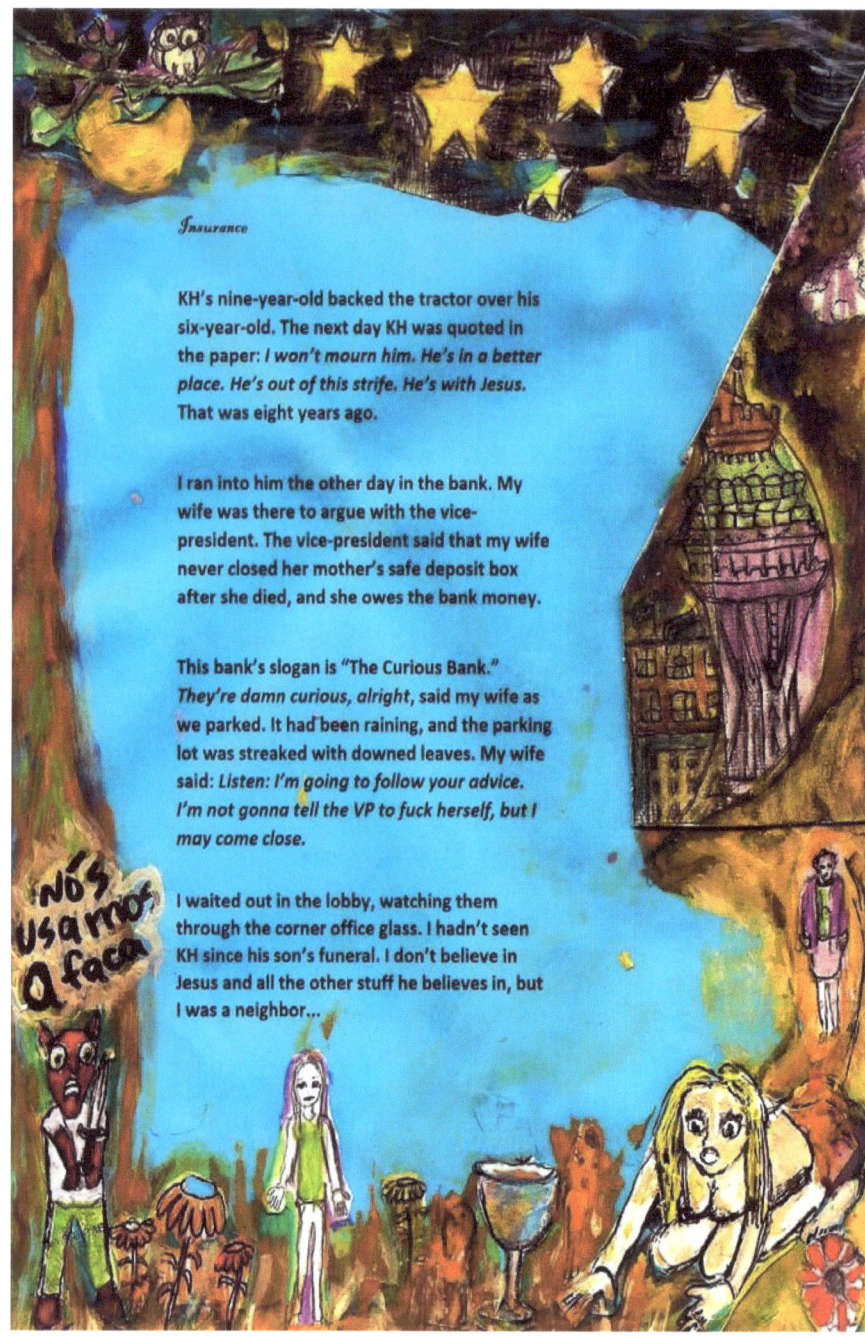

Insurance

KH's nine-year-old backed the tractor over his six-year-old. The next day KH was quoted in the paper: *I won't mourn him. He's in a better place. He's out of this strife. He's with Jesus.* That was eight years ago.

I ran into him the other day in the bank. My wife was there to argue with the vice-president. The vice-president said that my wife never closed her mother's safe deposit box after she died, and she owes the bank money.

This bank's slogan is "The Curious Bank." *They're damn curious, alright*, said my wife as we parked. It had been raining, and the parking lot was streaked with downed leaves. My wife said: *Listen: I'm going to follow your advice. I'm not gonna tell the VP to fuck herself, but I may come close.*

I waited out in the lobby, watching them through the corner office glass. I hadn't seen KH since his son's funeral. I don't believe in Jesus and all the other stuff he believes in, but I was a neighbor...

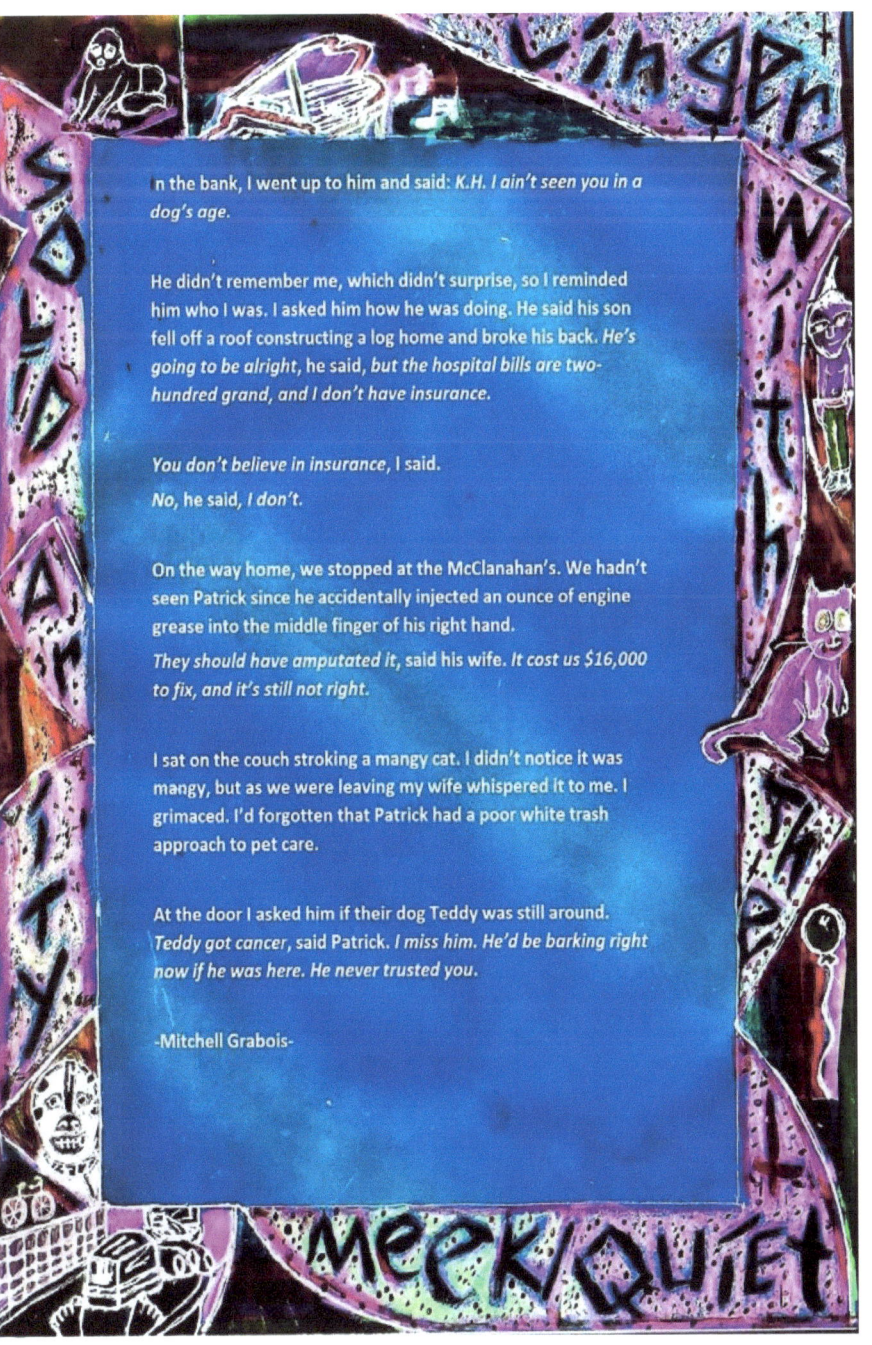

in the bank, I went up to him and said: *K.H. I ain't seen you in a dog's age.*

He didn't remember me, which didn't surprise, so I reminded him who I was. I asked him how he was doing. He said his son fell off a roof constructing a log home and broke his back. *He's going to be alright*, he said, *but the hospital bills are two-hundred grand, and I don't have insurance.*

You don't believe in insurance, I said.
No, he said, *I don't.*

On the way home, we stopped at the McClanahan's. We hadn't seen Patrick since he accidentally injected an ounce of engine grease into the middle finger of his right hand.
They should have amputated it, said his wife. *It cost us $16,000 to fix, and it's still not right.*

I sat on the couch stroking a mangy cat. I didn't notice it was mangy, but as we were leaving my wife whispered it to me. I grimaced. I'd forgotten that Patrick had a poor white trash approach to pet care.

At the door I asked him if their dog Teddy was still around. *Teddy got cancer*, said Patrick. *I miss him. He'd be barking right now if he was here. He never trusted you.*

-Mitchell Grabois-

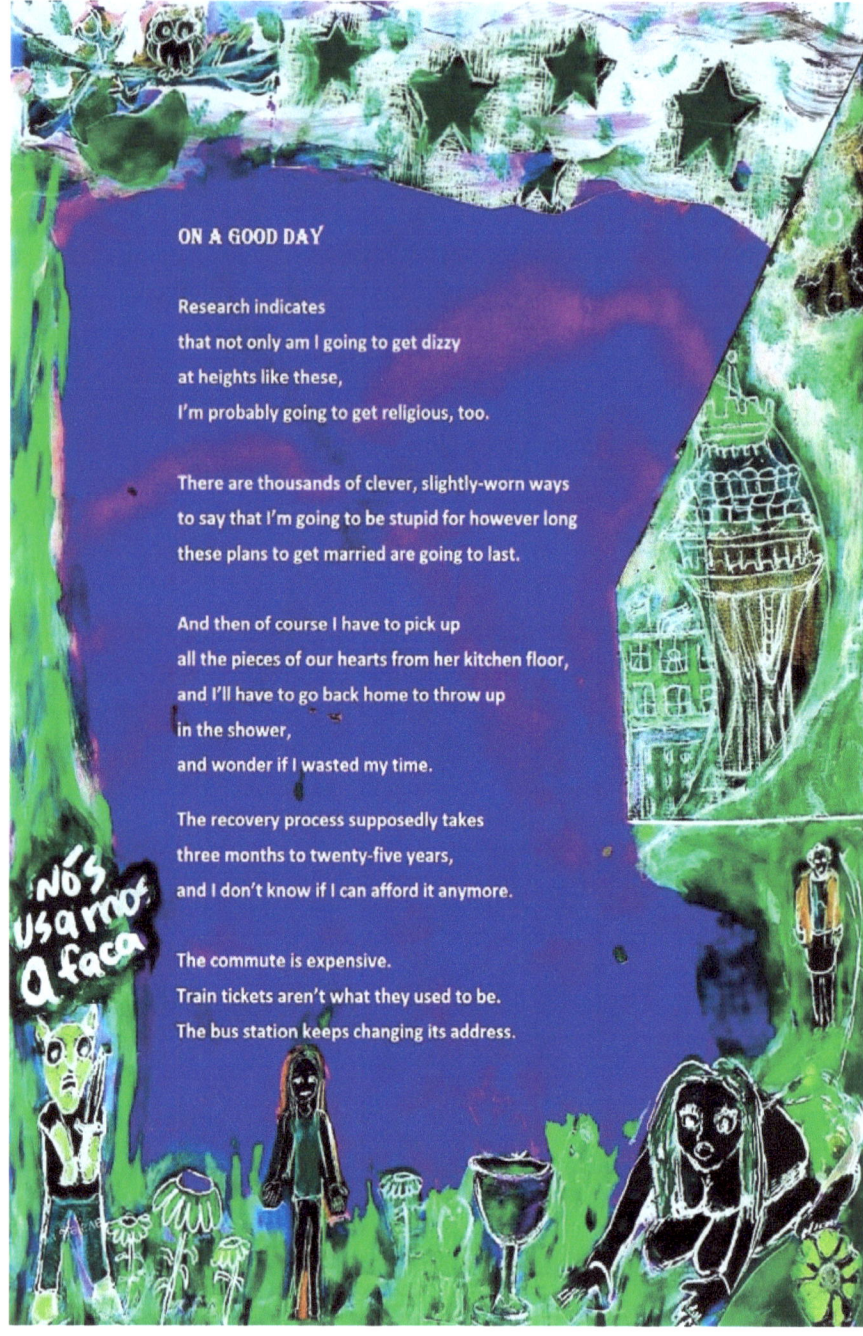

ON A GOOD DAY

Research indicates
that not only am I going to get dizzy
at heights like these,
I'm probably going to get religious, too.

There are thousands of clever, slightly-worn ways
to say that I'm going to be stupid for however long
these plans to get married are going to last.

And then of course I have to pick up
all the pieces of our hearts from her kitchen floor,
and I'll have to go back home to throw up
in the shower,
and wonder if I wasted my time.

The recovery process supposedly takes
three months to twenty-five years,
and I don't know if I can afford it anymore.

The commute is expensive.
Train tickets aren't what they used to be.
The bus station keeps changing its address.

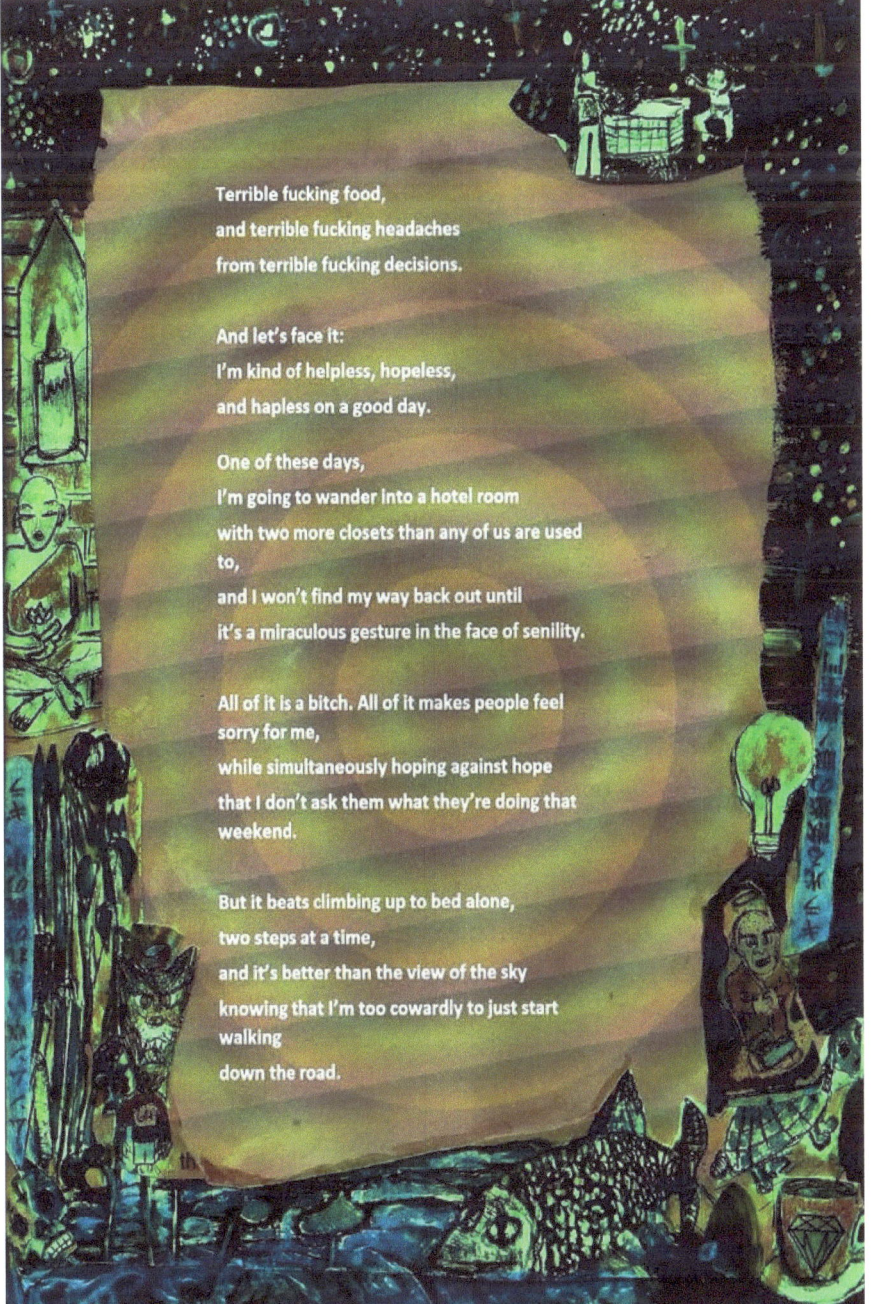

Terrible fucking food,
and terrible fucking headaches
from terrible fucking decisions.

And let's face it:
I'm kind of helpless, hopeless,
and hapless on a good day.

One of these days,
I'm going to wander into a hotel room
with two more closets than any of us are used
to,
and I won't find my way back out until
it's a miraculous gesture in the face of senility.

All of it is a bitch. All of it makes people feel
sorry for me,
while simultaneously hoping against hope
that I don't ask them what they're doing that
weekend.

But it beats climbing up to bed alone,
two steps at a time,
and it's better than the view of the sky
knowing that I'm too cowardly to just start
walking
down the road.

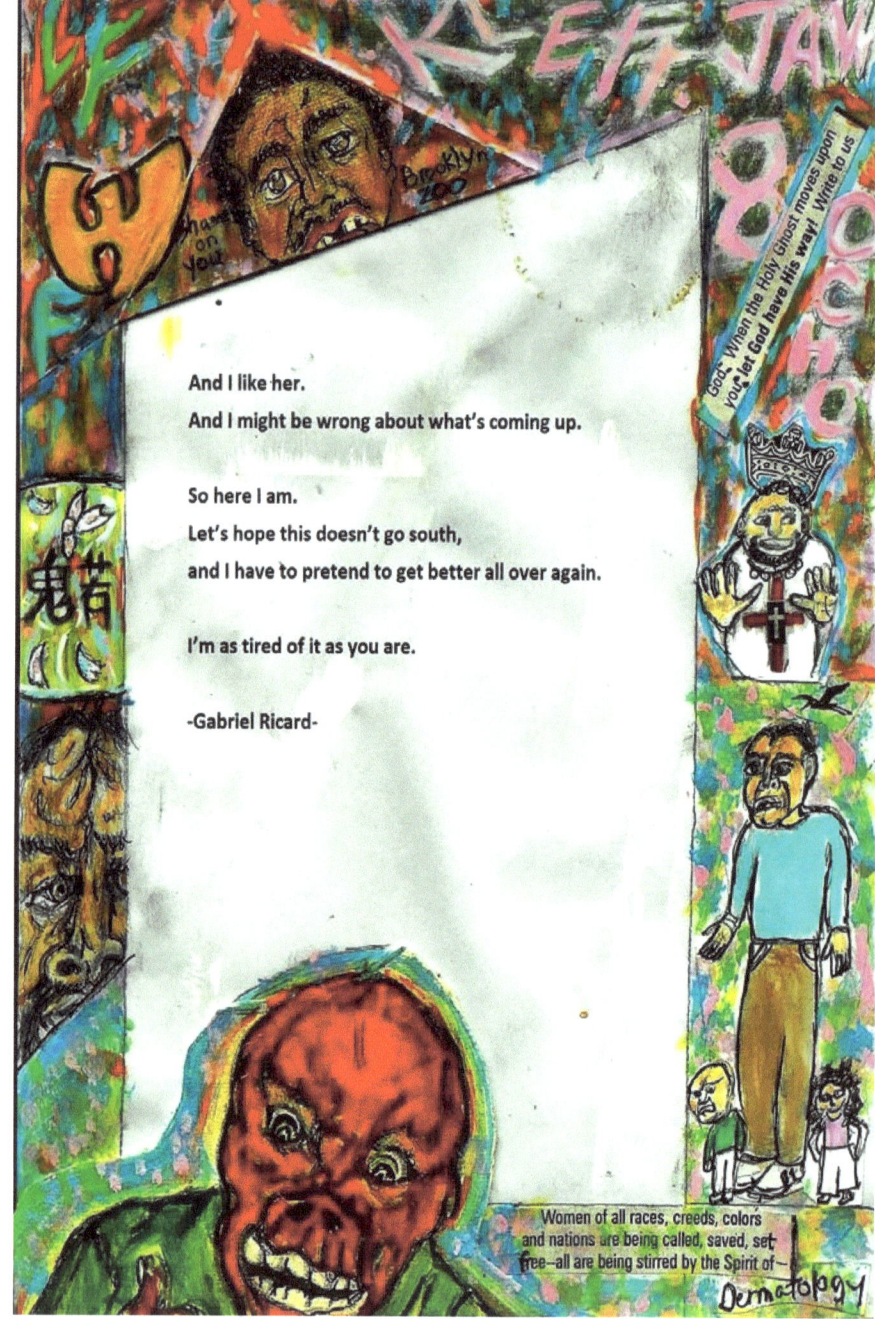

And I like her.

And I might be wrong about what's coming up.

So here I am.

Let's hope this doesn't go south,

and I have to pretend to get better all over again.

I'm as tired of it as you are.

-Gabriel Ricard-

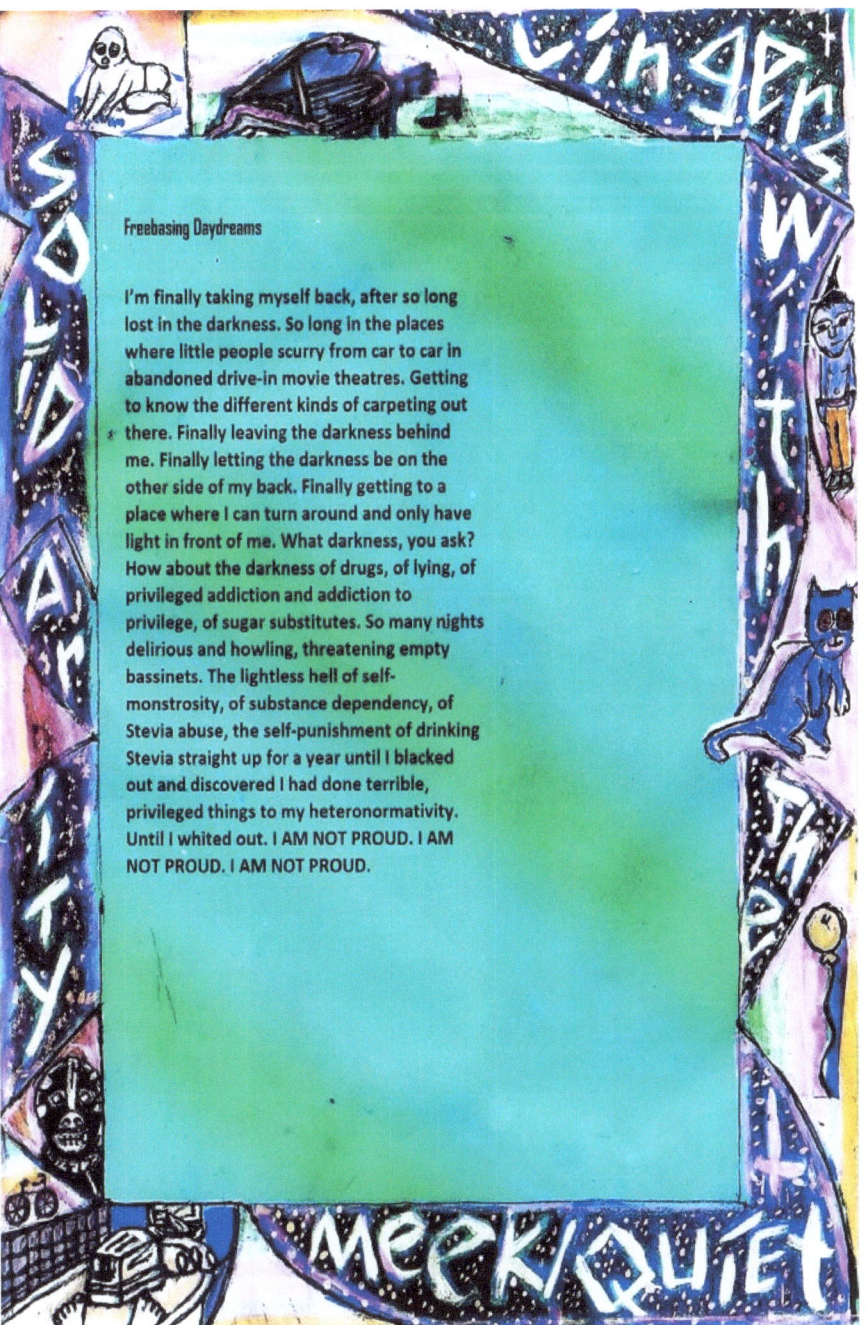

Freebasing Daydreams

I'm finally taking myself back, after so long lost in the darkness. So long in the places where little people scurry from car to car in abandoned drive-in movie theatres. Getting to know the different kinds of carpeting out there. Finally leaving the darkness behind me. Finally letting the darkness be on the other side of my back. Finally getting to a place where I can turn around and only have light in front of me. What darkness, you ask? How about the darkness of drugs, of lying, of privileged addiction and addiction to privilege, of sugar substitutes. So many nights delirious and howling, threatening empty bassinets. The lightless hell of self-monstrosity, of substance dependency, of Stevia abuse, the self-punishment of drinking Stevia straight up for a year until I blacked out and discovered I had done terrible, privileged things to my heteronormativity. Until I whited out. I AM NOT PROUD. I AM NOT PROUD. I AM NOT PROUD.

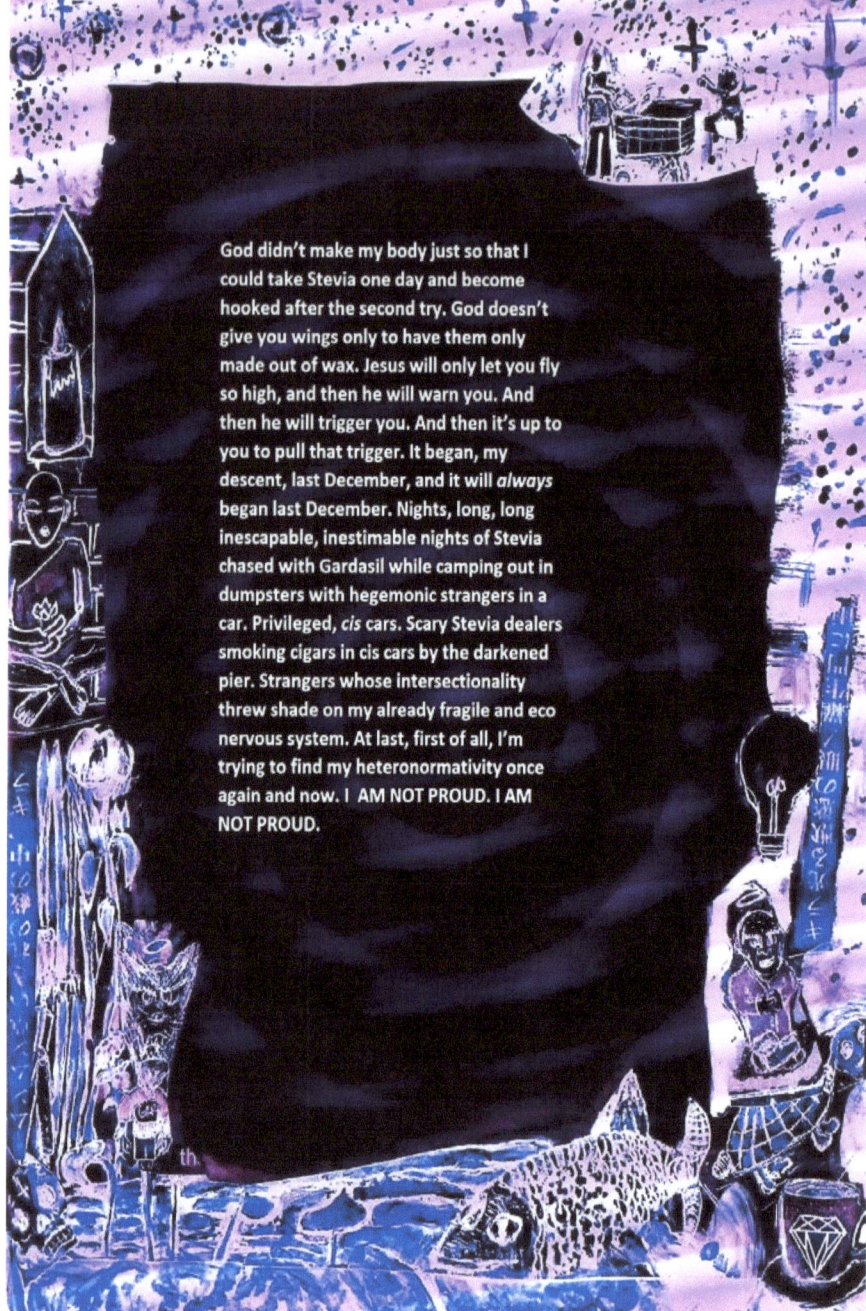

God didn't make my body just so that I could take Stevia one day and become hooked after the second try. God doesn't give you wings only to have them only made out of wax. Jesus will only let you fly so high, and then he will warn you. And then he will trigger you. And then it's up to you to pull that trigger. It began, my descent, last December, and it will *always* began last December. Nights, long, long inescapable, inestimable nights of Stevia chased with Gardasil while camping out in dumpsters with hegemonic strangers in a car. Privileged, *cis* cars. Scary Stevia dealers smoking cigars in cis cars by the darkened pier. Strangers whose intersectionality threw shade on my already fragile and eco nervous system. At last, first of all, I'm trying to find my heteronormativity once again and now. I AM NOT PROUD. I AM NOT PROUD.

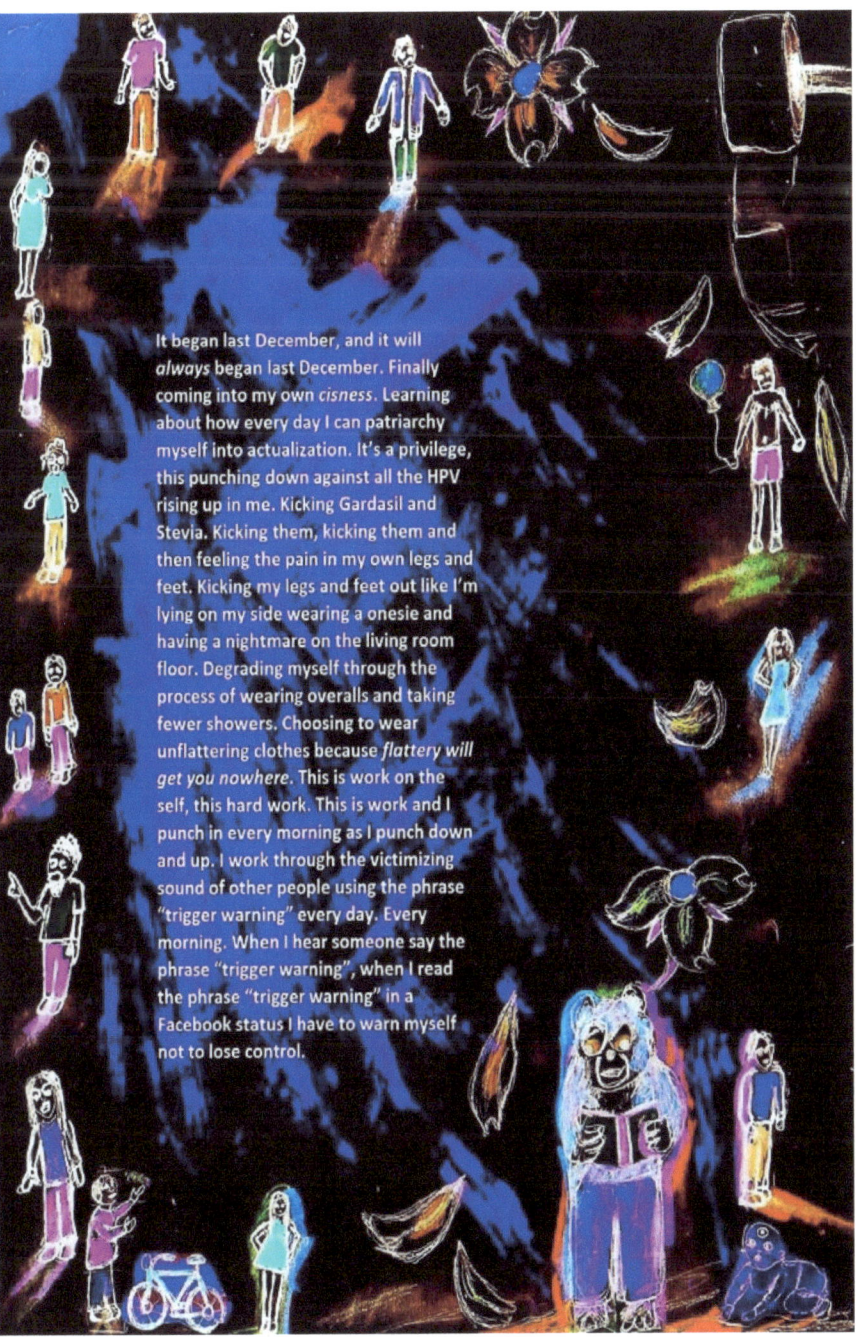

It began last December, and it will *always* began last December. Finally coming into my own *cisness*. Learning about how every day I can patriarchy myself into actualization. It's a privilege, this punching down against all the HPV rising up in me. Kicking Gardasil and Stevia. Kicking them, kicking them and then feeling the pain in my own legs and feet. Kicking my legs and feet out like I'm lying on my side wearing a onesie and having a nightmare on the living room floor. Degrading myself through the process of wearing overalls and taking fewer showers. Choosing to wear unflattering clothes because *flattery will get you nowhere*. This is work on the self, this hard work. This is work and I punch in every morning as I punch down and up. I work through the victimizing sound of other people using the phrase "trigger warning" every day. Every morning. When I hear someone say the phrase "trigger warning", when I read the phrase "trigger warning" in a Facebook status I have to warn myself not to lose control.

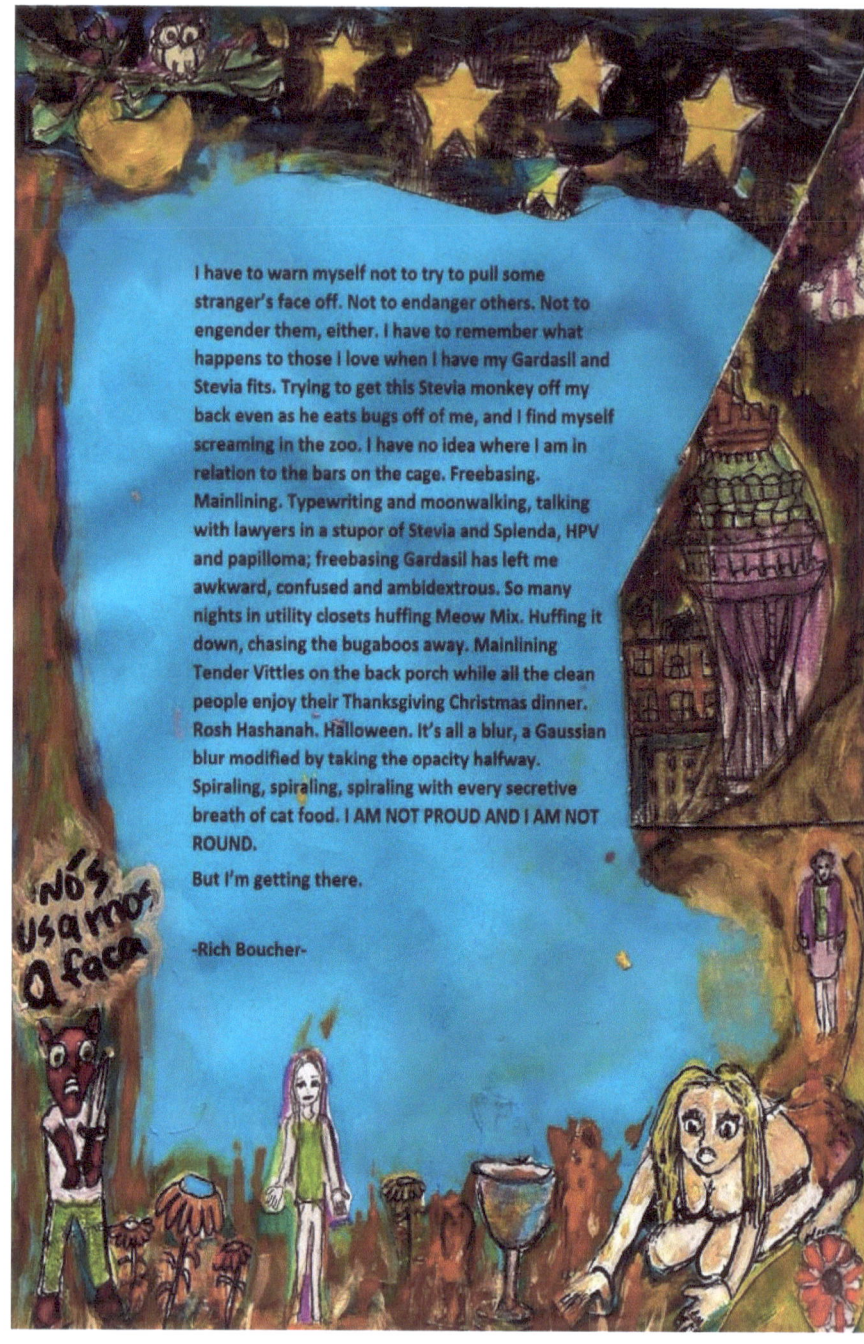

I have to warn myself not to try to pull some stranger's face off. Not to endanger others. Not to engender them, either. I have to remember what happens to those I love when I have my Gardasil and Stevia fits. Trying to get this Stevia monkey off my back even as he eats bugs off of me, and I find myself screaming in the zoo. I have no idea where I am in relation to the bars on the cage. Freebasing. Mainlining. Typewriting and moonwalking, talking with lawyers in a stupor of Stevia and Splenda, HPV and papilloma; freebasing Gardasil has left me awkward, confused and ambidextrous. So many nights in utility closets huffing Meow Mix. Huffing it down, chasing the bugaboos away. Mainlining Tender Vittles on the back porch while all the clean people enjoy their Thanksgiving Christmas dinner. Rosh Hashanah. Halloween. It's all a blur, a Gaussian blur modified by taking the opacity halfway. Spiraling, spiraling, spiraling with every secretive breath of cat food. I AM NOT PROUD AND I AM NOT ROUND.

But I'm getting there.

-Rich Boucher-

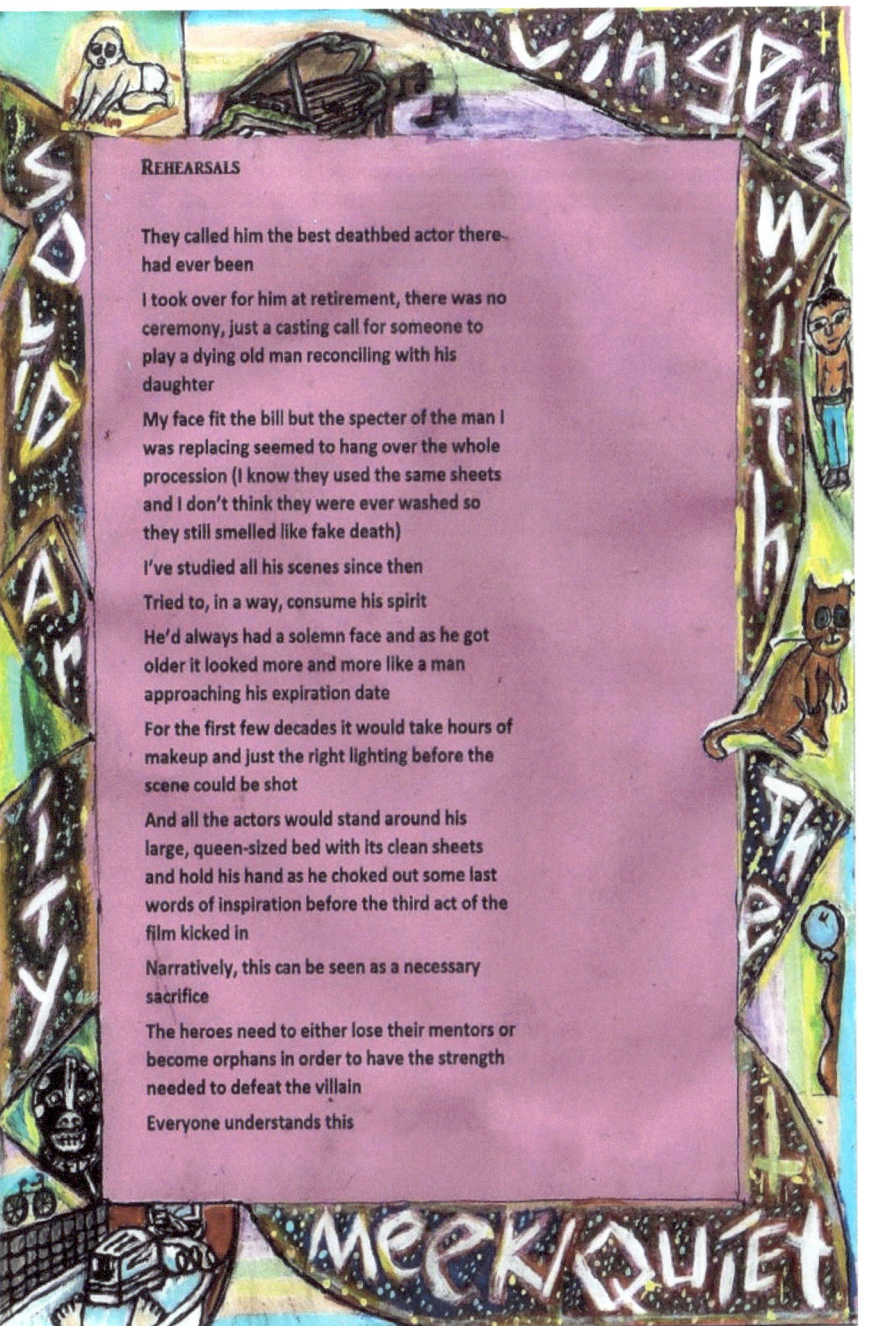

REHEARSALS

They called him the best deathbed actor there had ever been

I took over for him at retirement, there was no ceremony, just a casting call for someone to play a dying old man reconciling with his daughter

My face fit the bill but the specter of the man I was replacing seemed to hang over the whole procession (I know they used the same sheets and I don't think they were ever washed so they still smelled like fake death)

I've studied all his scenes since then

Tried to, in a way, consume his spirit

He'd always had a solemn face and as he got older it looked more and more like a man approaching his expiration date

For the first few decades it would take hours of makeup and just the right lighting before the scene could be shot

And all the actors would stand around his large, queen-sized bed with its clean sheets and hold his hand as he choked out some last words of inspiration before the third act of the film kicked in

Narratively, this can be seen as a necessary sacrifice

The heroes need to either lose their mentors or become orphans in order to have the strength needed to defeat the villain

Everyone understands this

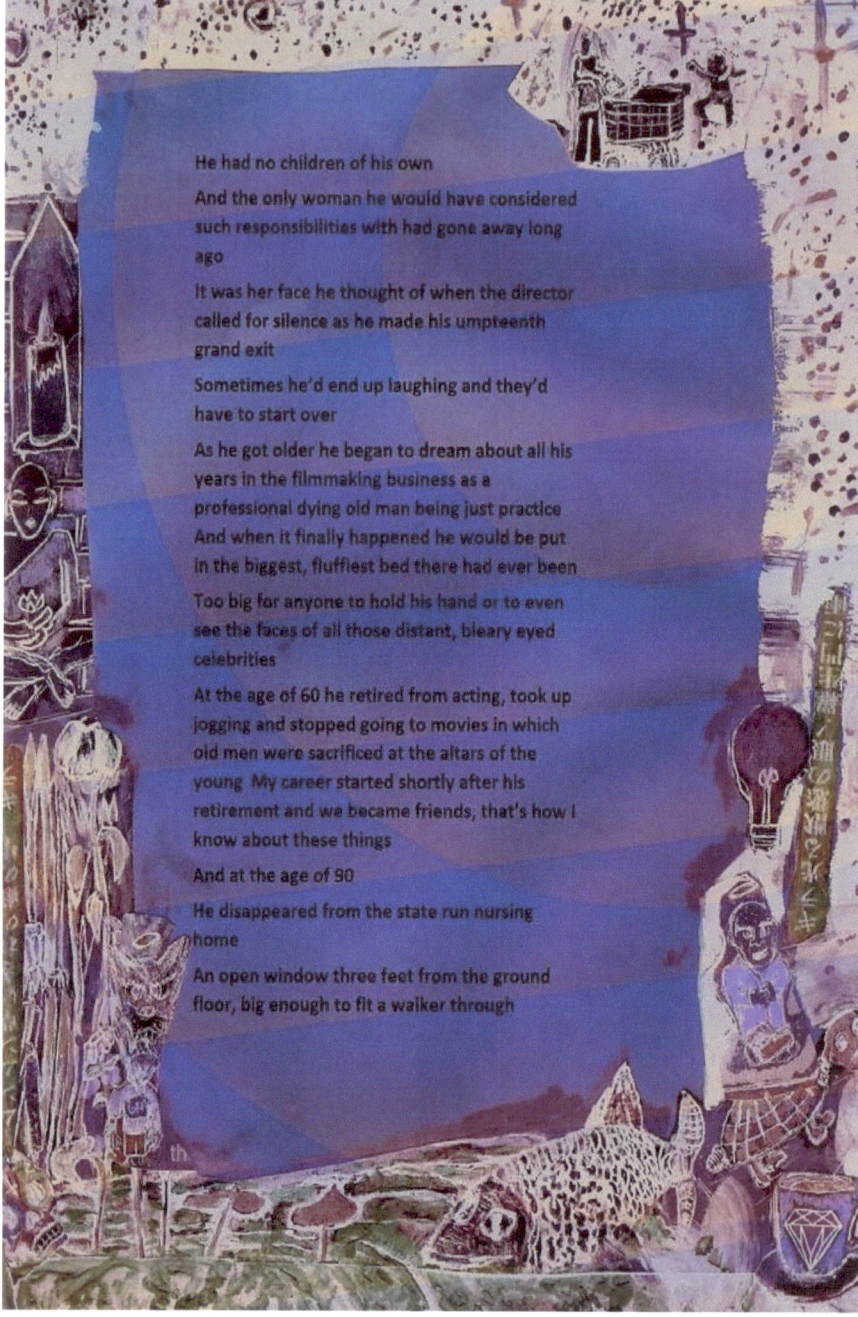

He had no children of his own

And the only woman he would have considered such responsibilities with had gone away long ago

It was her face he thought of when the director called for silence as he made his umpteenth grand exit

Sometimes he'd end up laughing and they'd have to start over

As he got older he began to dream about all his years in the filmmaking business as a professional dying old man being just practice And when it finally happened he would be put in the biggest, fluffiest bed there had ever been

Too big for anyone to hold his hand or to even see the faces of all those distant, bleary eyed celebrities

At the age of 60 he retired from acting, took up jogging and stopped going to movies in which old men were sacrificed at the altars of the young My career started shortly after his retirement and we became friends, that's how I know about these things

And at the age of 90

He disappeared from the state run nursing home

An open window three feet from the ground floor, big enough to fit a walker through

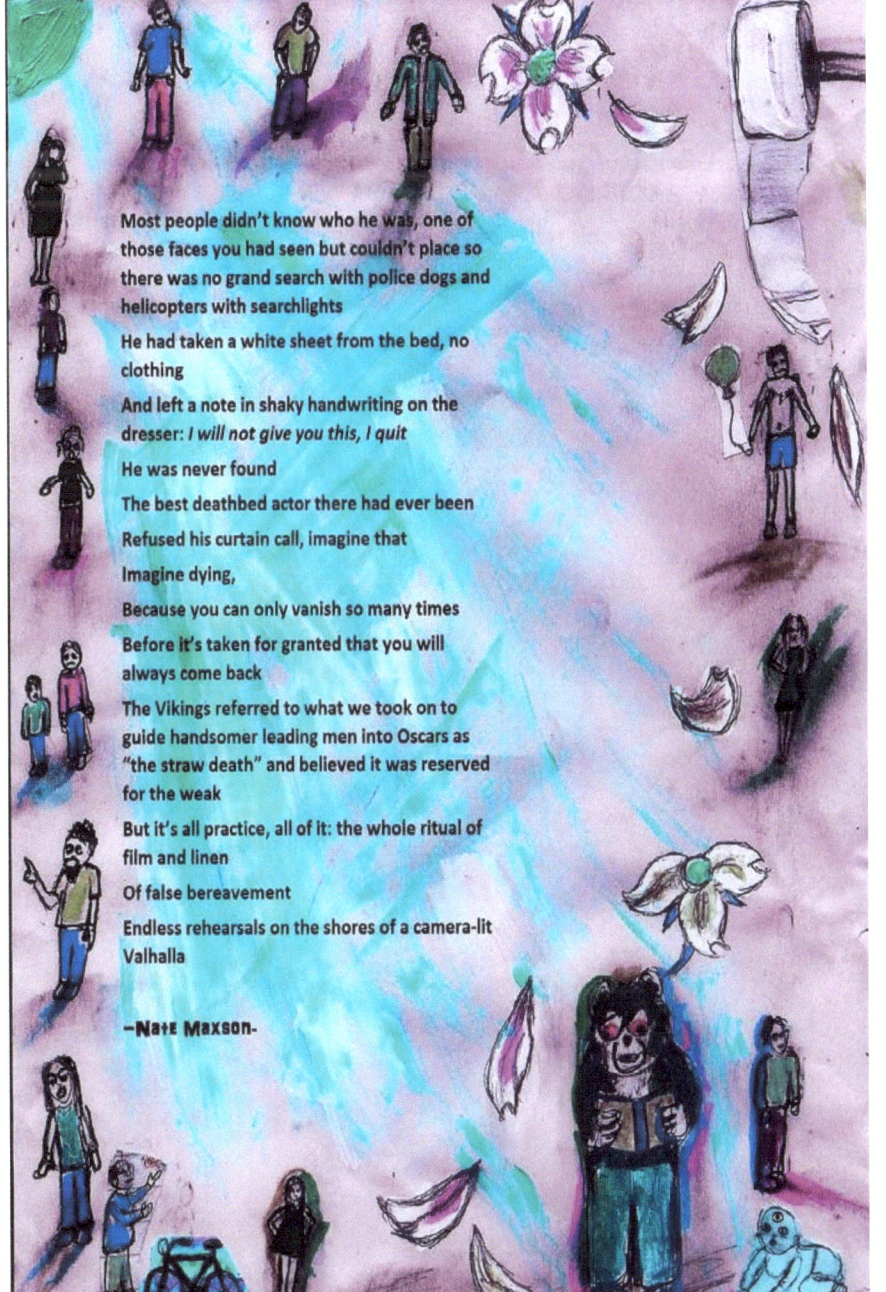

Most people didn't know who he was, one of those faces you had seen but couldn't place so there was no grand search with police dogs and helicopters with searchlights

He had taken a white sheet from the bed, no clothing

And left a note in shaky handwriting on the dresser: *I will not give you this, I quit*

He was never found

The best deathbed actor there had ever been

Refused his curtain call, imagine that

Imagine dying,

Because you can only vanish so many times

Before it's taken for granted that you will always come back

The Vikings referred to what we took on to guide handsomer leading men into Oscars as "the straw death" and believed it was reserved for the weak

But it's all practice, all of it: the whole ritual of film and linen

Of false bereavement

Endless rehearsals on the shores of a camera-lit Valhalla

—Nate Maxson—

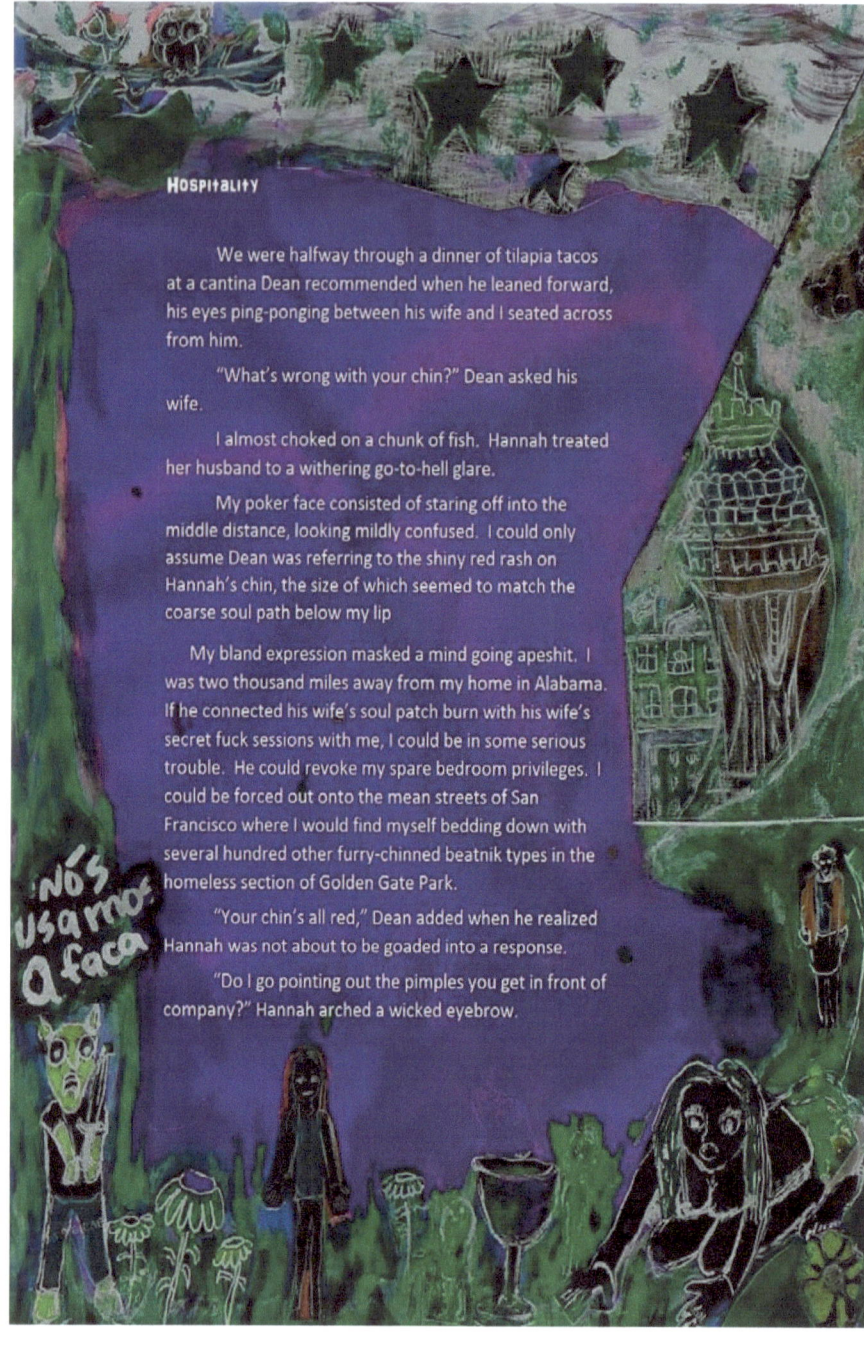

HOSPITALITY

We were halfway through a dinner of tilapia tacos at a cantina Dean recommended when he leaned forward, his eyes ping-ponging between his wife and I seated across from him.

"What's wrong with your chin?" Dean asked his wife.

I almost choked on a chunk of fish. Hannah treated her husband to a withering go-to-hell glare.

My poker face consisted of staring off into the middle distance, looking mildly confused. I could only assume Dean was referring to the shiny red rash on Hannah's chin, the size of which seemed to match the coarse soul path below my lip

My bland expression masked a mind going apeshit. I was two thousand miles away from my home in Alabama. If he connected his wife's soul patch burn with his wife's secret fuck sessions with me, I could be in some serious trouble. He could revoke my spare bedroom privileges. I could be forced out onto the mean streets of San Francisco where I would find myself bedding down with several hundred other furry-chinned beatnik types in the homeless section of Golden Gate Park.

"Your chin's all red," Dean added when he realized Hannah was not about to be goaded into a response.

"Do I go pointing out the pimples you get in front of company?" Hannah arched a wicked eyebrow.

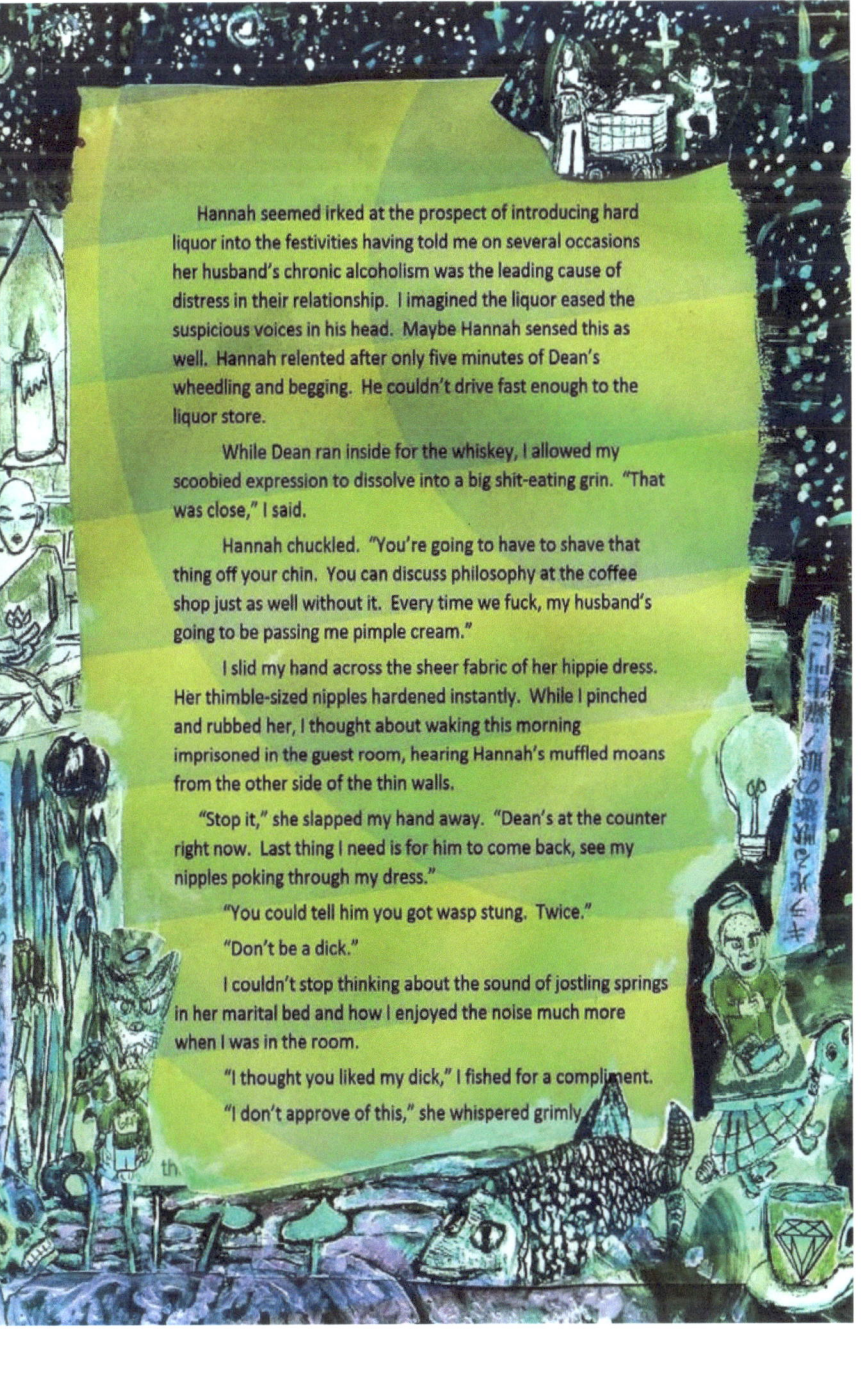

Hannah seemed irked at the prospect of introducing hard liquor into the festivities having told me on several occasions her husband's chronic alcoholism was the leading cause of distress in their relationship. I imagined the liquor eased the suspicious voices in his head. Maybe Hannah sensed this as well. Hannah relented after only five minutes of Dean's wheedling and begging. He couldn't drive fast enough to the liquor store.

While Dean ran inside for the whiskey, I allowed my scoobied expression to dissolve into a big shit-eating grin. "That was close," I said.

Hannah chuckled. "You're going to have to shave that thing off your chin. You can discuss philosophy at the coffee shop just as well without it. Every time we fuck, my husband's going to be passing me pimple cream."

I slid my hand across the sheer fabric of her hippie dress. Her thimble-sized nipples hardened instantly. While I pinched and rubbed her, I thought about waking this morning imprisoned in the guest room, hearing Hannah's muffled moans from the other side of the thin walls.

"Stop it," she slapped my hand away. "Dean's at the counter right now. Last thing I need is for him to come back, see my nipples poking through my dress."

"You could tell him you got wasp stung. Twice."

"Don't be a dick."

I couldn't stop thinking about the sound of jostling springs in her marital bed and how I enjoyed the noise much more when I was in the room.

"I thought you liked my dick," I fished for a compliment.

"I don't approve of this," she whispered grimly.

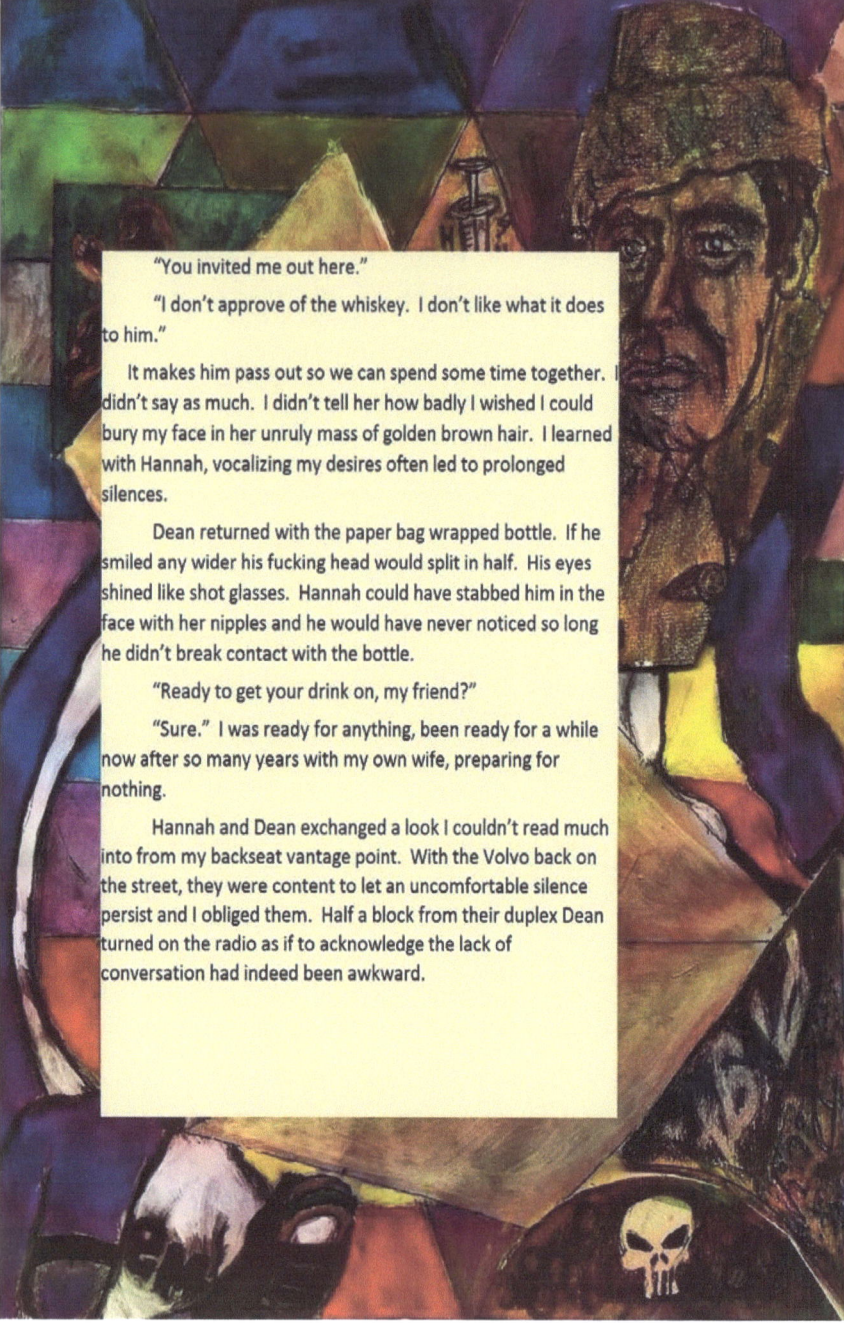

"You invited me out here."

"I don't approve of the whiskey. I don't like what it does to him."

It makes him pass out so we can spend some time together. I didn't say as much. I didn't tell her how badly I wished I could bury my face in her unruly mass of golden brown hair. I learned with Hannah, vocalizing my desires often led to prolonged silences.

Dean returned with the paper bag wrapped bottle. If he smiled any wider his fucking head would split in half. His eyes shined like shot glasses. Hannah could have stabbed him in the face with her nipples and he would have never noticed so long he didn't break contact with the bottle.

"Ready to get your drink on, my friend?"

"Sure." I was ready for anything, been ready for a while now after so many years with my own wife, preparing for nothing.

Hannah and Dean exchanged a look I couldn't read much into from my backseat vantage point. With the Volvo back on the street, they were content to let an uncomfortable silence persist and I obliged them. Half a block from their duplex Dean turned on the radio as if to acknowledge the lack of conversation had indeed been awkward.

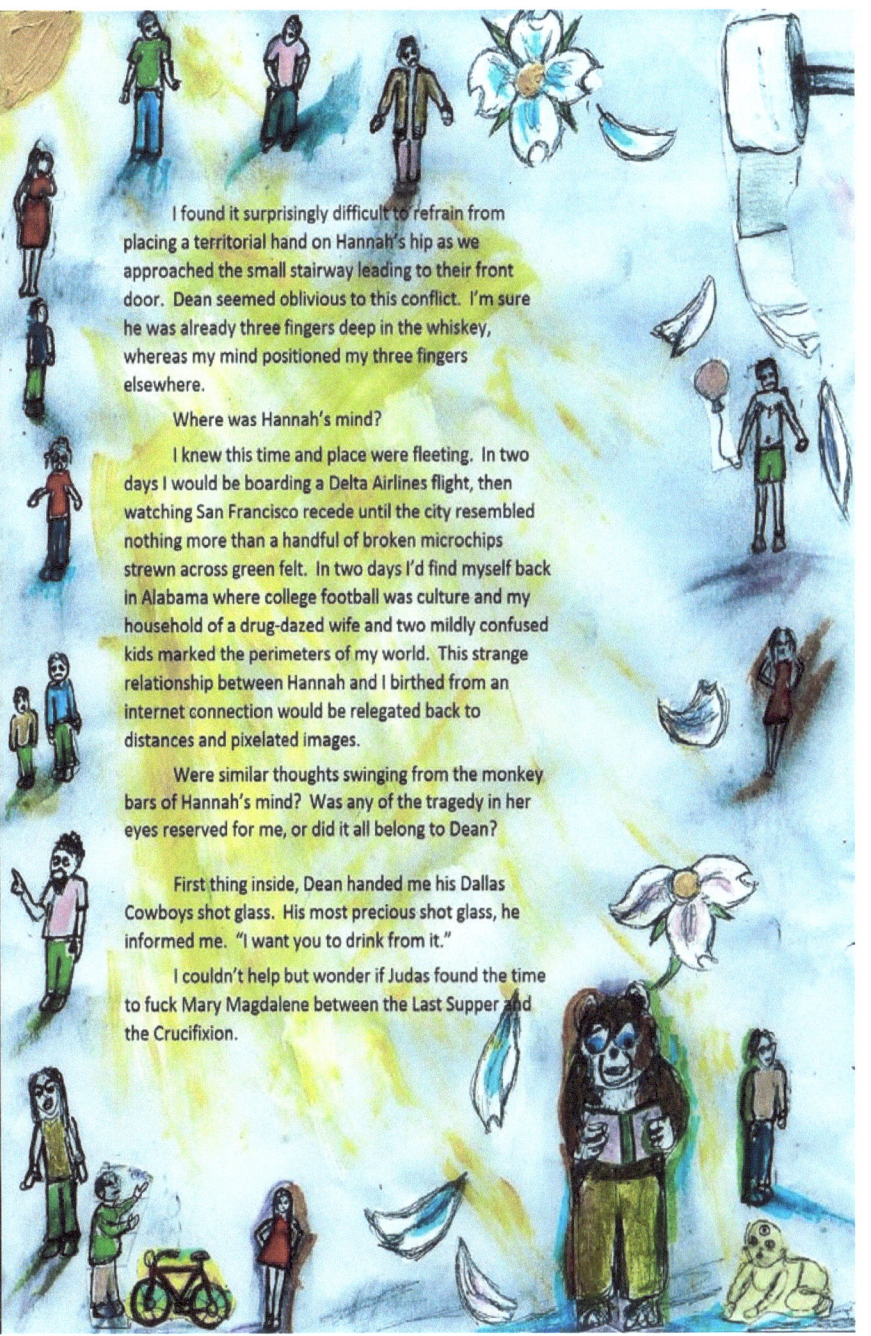

I found it surprisingly difficult to refrain from placing a territorial hand on Hannah's hip as we approached the small stairway leading to their front door. Dean seemed oblivious to this conflict. I'm sure he was already three fingers deep in the whiskey, whereas my mind positioned my three fingers elsewhere.

Where was Hannah's mind?

I knew this time and place were fleeting. In two days I would be boarding a Delta Airlines flight, then watching San Francisco recede until the city resembled nothing more than a handful of broken microchips strewn across green felt. In two days I'd find myself back in Alabama where college football was culture and my household of a drug-dazed wife and two mildly confused kids marked the perimeters of my world. This strange relationship between Hannah and I birthed from an internet connection would be relegated back to distances and pixelated images.

Were similar thoughts swinging from the monkey bars of Hannah's mind? Was any of the tragedy in her eyes reserved for me, or did it all belong to Dean?

First thing inside, Dean handed me his Dallas Cowboys shot glass. His most precious shot glass, he informed me. "I want you to drink from it."

I couldn't help but wonder if Judas found the time to fuck Mary Magdalene between the Last Supper and the Crucifixion.

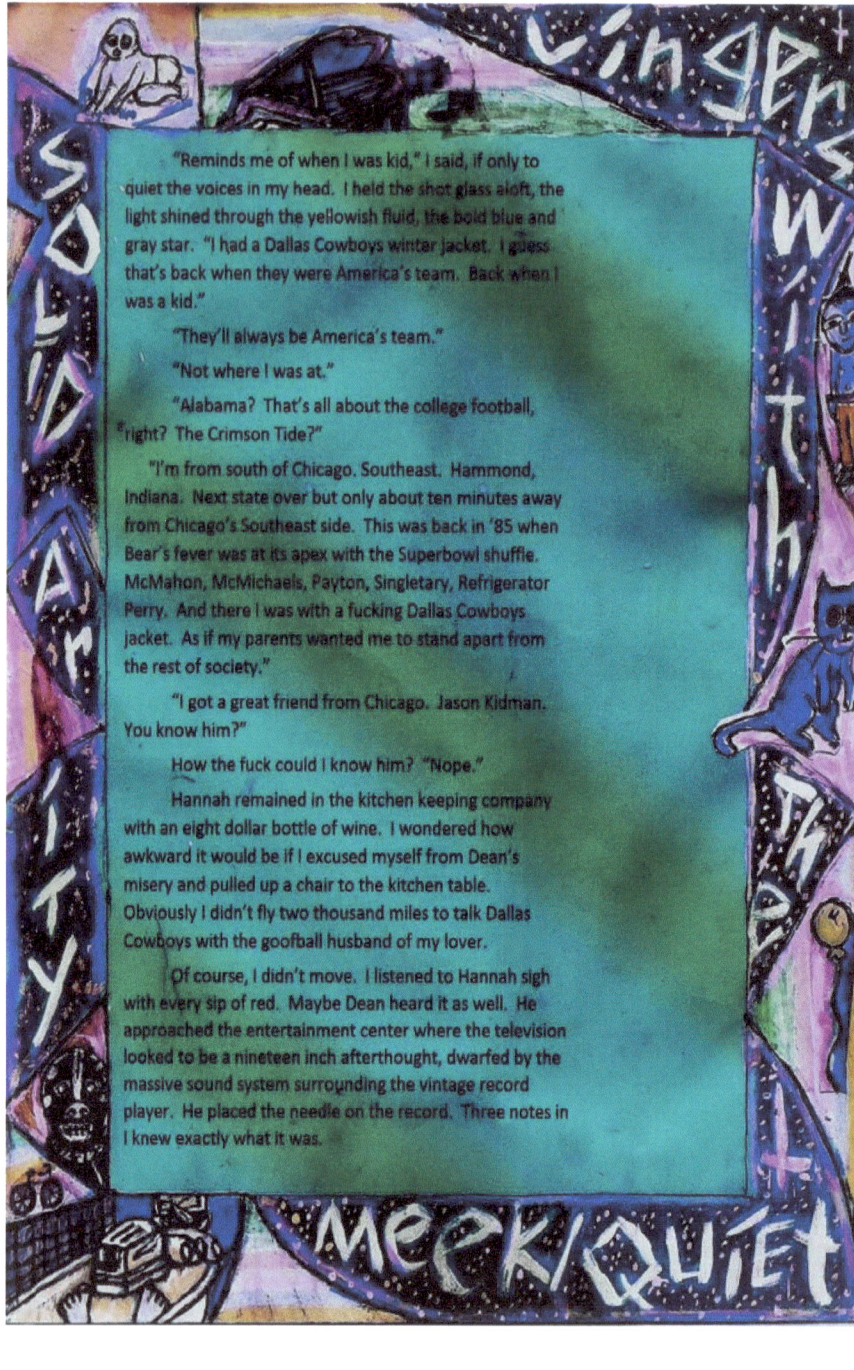

"Reminds me of when I was kid," I said, if only to quiet the voices in my head. I held the shot glass aloft, the light shined through the yellowish fluid, the bold blue and gray star. "I had a Dallas Cowboys winter jacket. I guess that's back when they were America's team. Back when I was a kid."

"They'll always be America's team."

"Not where I was at."

"Alabama? That's all about the college football, right? The Crimson Tide?"

"I'm from south of Chicago. Southeast. Hammond, Indiana. Next state over but only about ten minutes away from Chicago's Southeast side. This was back in '85 when Bear's fever was at its apex with the Superbowl shuffle. McMahon, McMichaels, Payton, Singletary, Refrigerator Perry. And there I was with a fucking Dallas Cowboys jacket. As if my parents wanted me to stand apart from the rest of society."

"I got a great friend from Chicago. Jason Kidman. You know him?"

How the fuck could I know him? "Nope."

Hannah remained in the kitchen keeping company with an eight dollar bottle of wine. I wondered how awkward it would be if I excused myself from Dean's misery and pulled up a chair to the kitchen table. Obviously I didn't fly two thousand miles to talk Dallas Cowboys with the goofball husband of my lover.

Of course, I didn't move. I listened to Hannah sigh with every sip of red. Maybe Dean heard it as well. He approached the entertainment center where the television looked to be a nineteen inch afterthought, dwarfed by the massive sound system surrounding the vintage record player. He placed the needle on the record. Three notes in I knew exactly what it was.

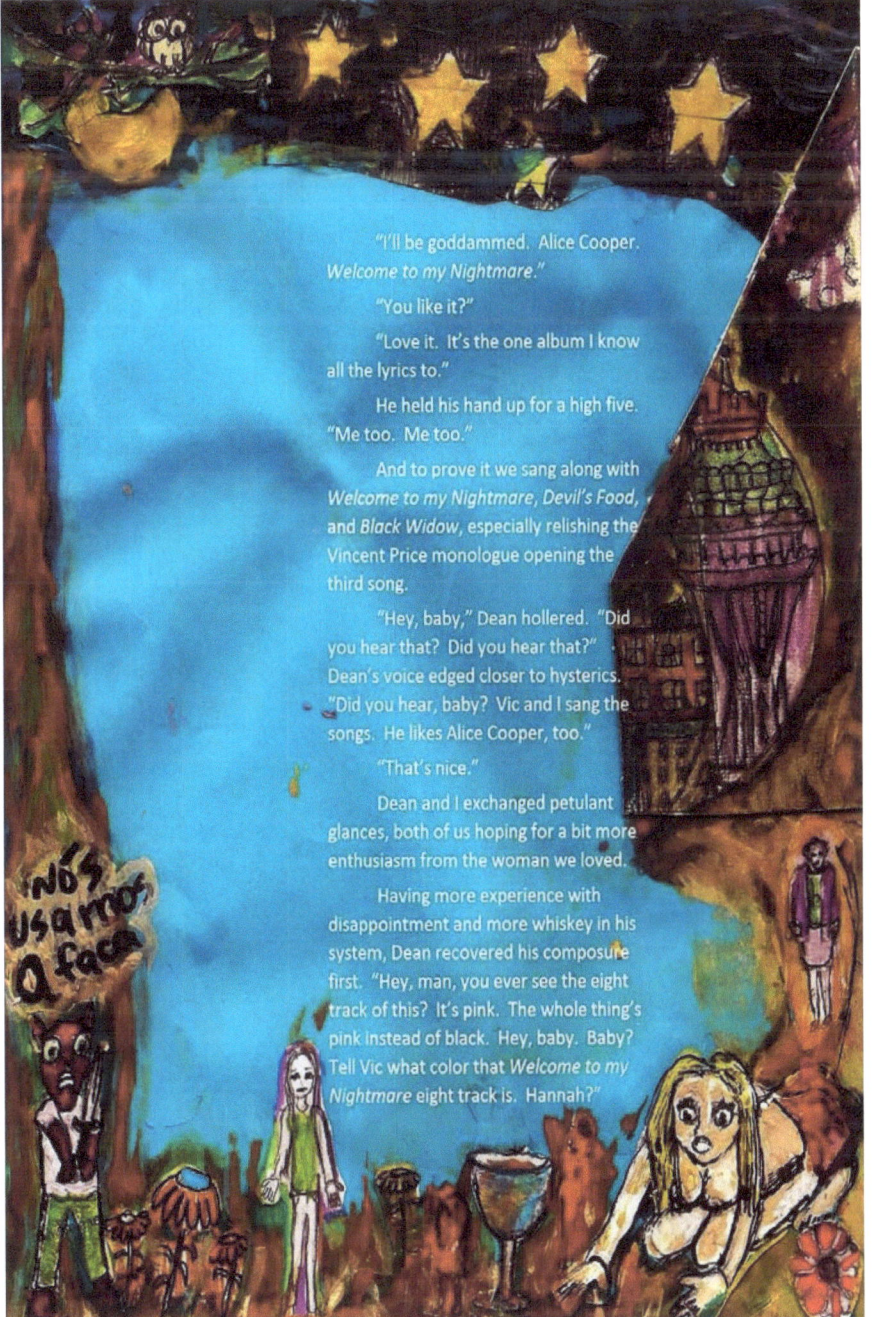

"I'll be goddammed. Alice Cooper. *Welcome to my Nightmare*."

"You like it?"

"Love it. It's the one album I know all the lyrics to."

He held his hand up for a high five. "Me too. Me too."

And to prove it we sang along with *Welcome to my Nightmare*, *Devil's Food*, and *Black Widow*, especially relishing the Vincent Price monologue opening the third song.

"Hey, baby," Dean hollered. "Did you hear that? Did you hear that?" Dean's voice edged closer to hysterics. "Did you hear, baby? Vic and I sang the songs. He likes Alice Cooper, too."

"That's nice."

Dean and I exchanged petulant glances, both of us hoping for a bit more enthusiasm from the woman we loved.

Having more experience with disappointment and more whiskey in his system, Dean recovered his composure first. "Hey, man, you ever see the eight track of this? It's pink. The whole thing's pink instead of black. Hey, baby. Baby? Tell Vic what color that *Welcome to my Nightmare* eight track is. Hannah?"

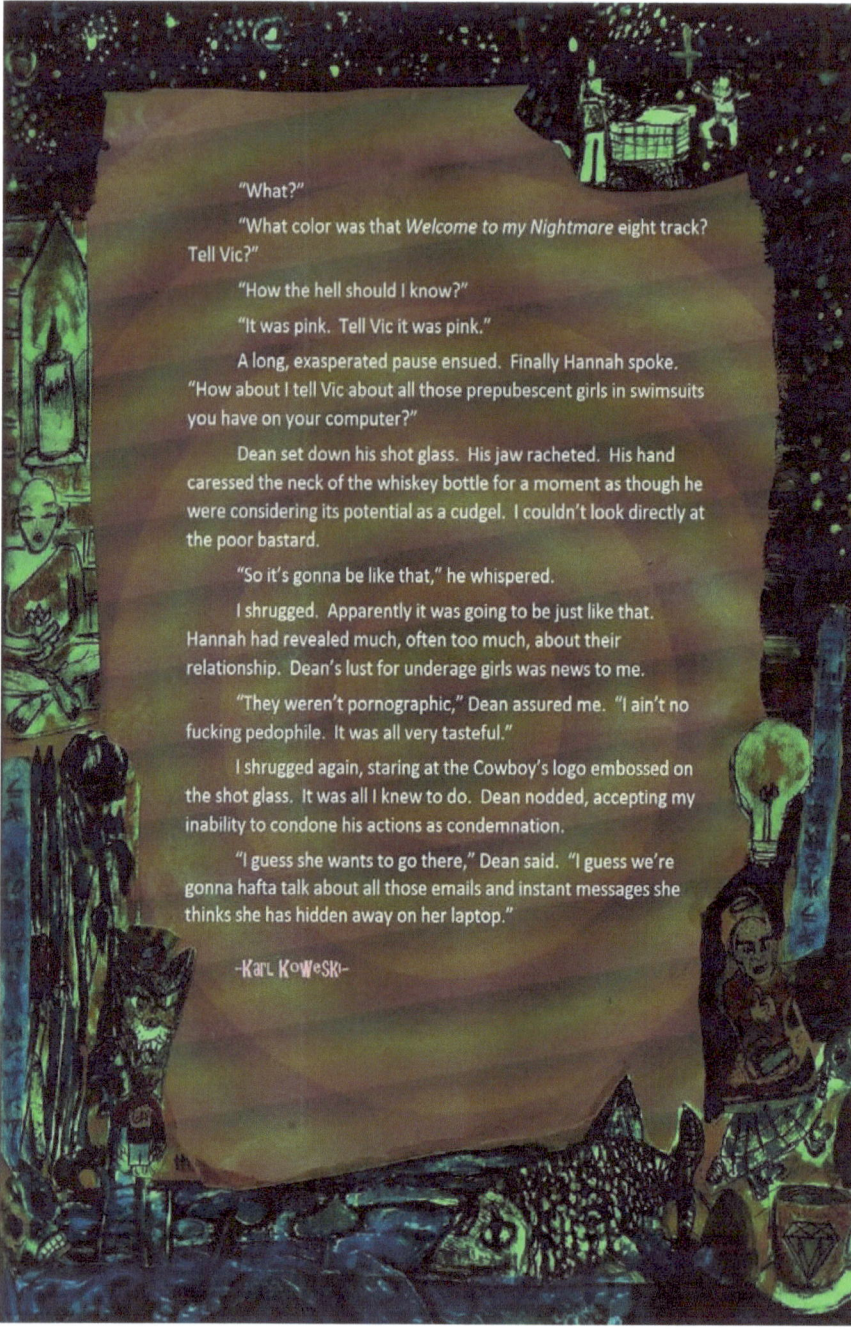

"What?"

"What color was that *Welcome to my Nightmare* eight track? Tell Vic?"

"How the hell should I know?"

"It was pink. Tell Vic it was pink."

A long, exasperated pause ensued. Finally Hannah spoke. "How about I tell Vic about all those prepubescent girls in swimsuits you have on your computer?"

Dean set down his shot glass. His jaw racheted. His hand caressed the neck of the whiskey bottle for a moment as though he were considering its potential as a cudgel. I couldn't look directly at the poor bastard.

"So it's gonna be like that," he whispered.

I shrugged. Apparently it was going to be just like that. Hannah had revealed much, often too much, about their relationship. Dean's lust for underage girls was news to me.

"They weren't pornographic," Dean assured me. "I ain't no fucking pedophile. It was all very tasteful."

I shrugged again, staring at the Cowboy's logo embossed on the shot glass. It was all I knew to do. Dean nodded, accepting my inability to condone his actions as condemnation.

"I guess she wants to go there," Dean said. "I guess we're gonna hafta talk about all those emails and instant messages she thinks she has hidden away on her laptop."

-Karl Koweski-

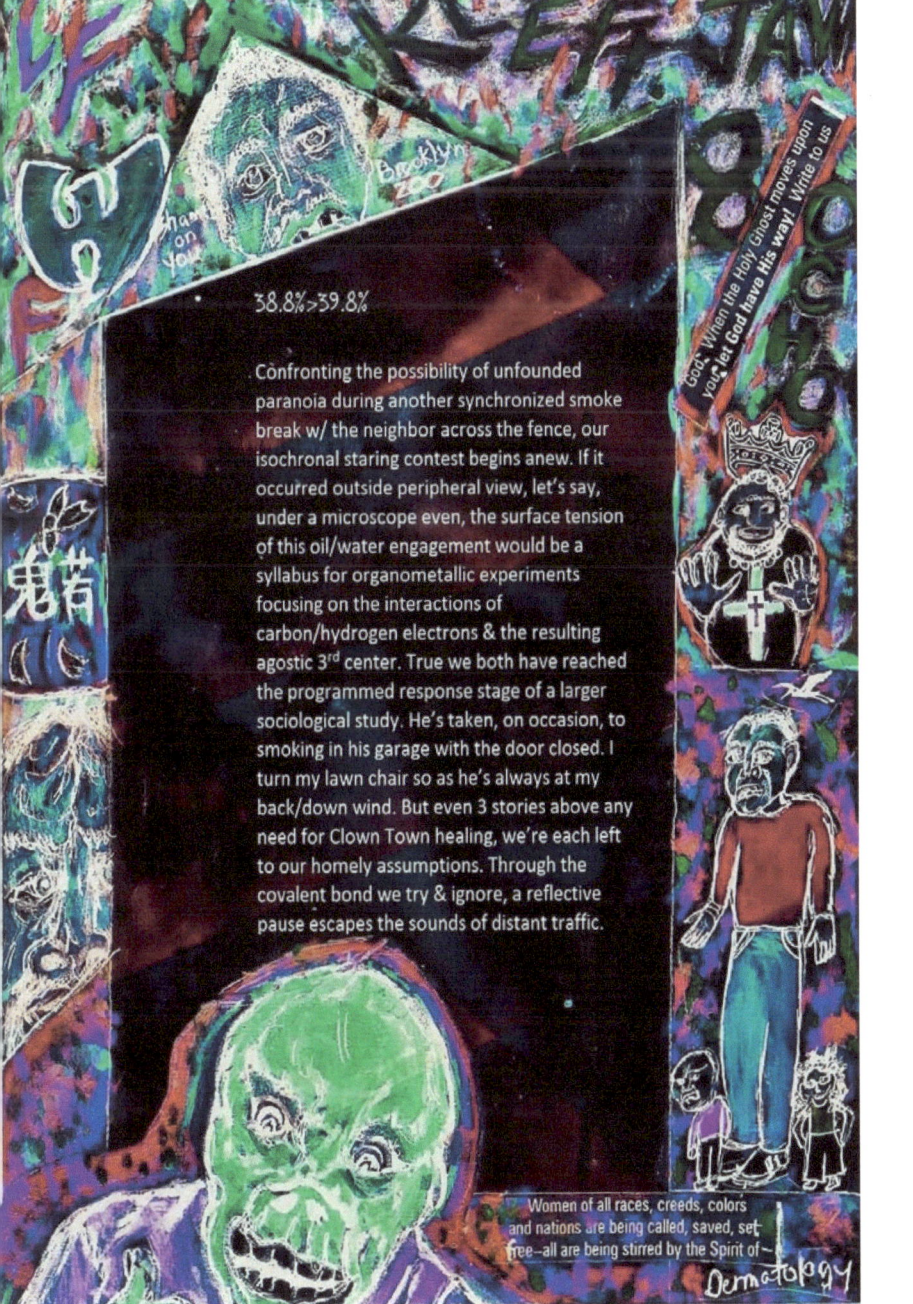

38.8%>39.8%

Confronting the possibility of unfounded paranoia during another synchronized smoke break w/ the neighbor across the fence, our isochronal staring contest begins anew. If it occurred outside peripheral view, let's say, under a microscope even, the surface tension of this oil/water engagement would be a syllabus for organometallic experiments focusing on the interactions of carbon/hydrogen electrons & the resulting agostic 3rd center. True we both have reached the programmed response stage of a larger sociological study. He's taken, on occasion, to smoking in his garage with the door closed. I turn my lawn chair so as he's always at my back/down wind. But even 3 stories above any need for Clown Town healing, we're each left to our homely assumptions. Through the covalent bond we try & ignore, a reflective pause escapes the sounds of distant traffic.

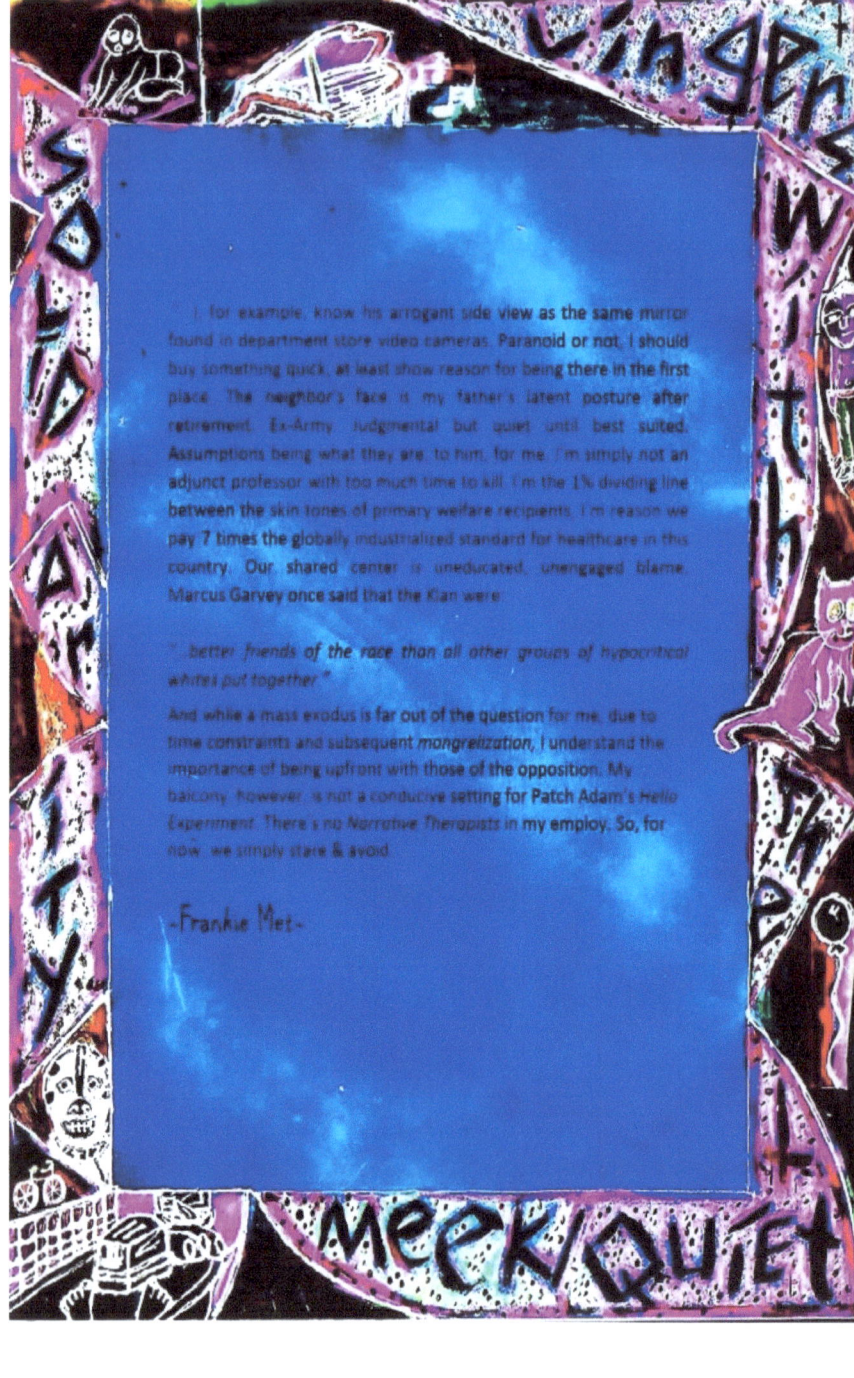

"...I, for example, know his arrogant side view as the same mirror found in department store video cameras. Paranoid or not, I should buy something quick, at least show reason for being there in the first place. The neighbor's face is my father's latent posture after retirement. Ex-Army, judgmental but quiet until best suited. Assumptions being what they are, to him, for me, I'm simply not an adjunct professor with too much time to kill. I'm the 1% dividing line between the skin tones of primary welfare recipients. I'm reason we pay 7 times the globally industrialized standard for healthcare in this country. Our shared center is uneducated, unengaged blame. Marcus Garvey once said that the Klan were

"...better friends of the race than all other groups of hypocritical whites put together."

And while a mass exodus is far out of the question for me, due to time constraints and subsequent *mongrelization*, I understand the importance of being upfront with those of the opposition. My balcony, however, is not a conducive setting for Patch Adam's *Hello Experiment*. There's no *Narrative Therapists* in my employ. So, for now, we simply stare & avoid.

-Frankie Met-

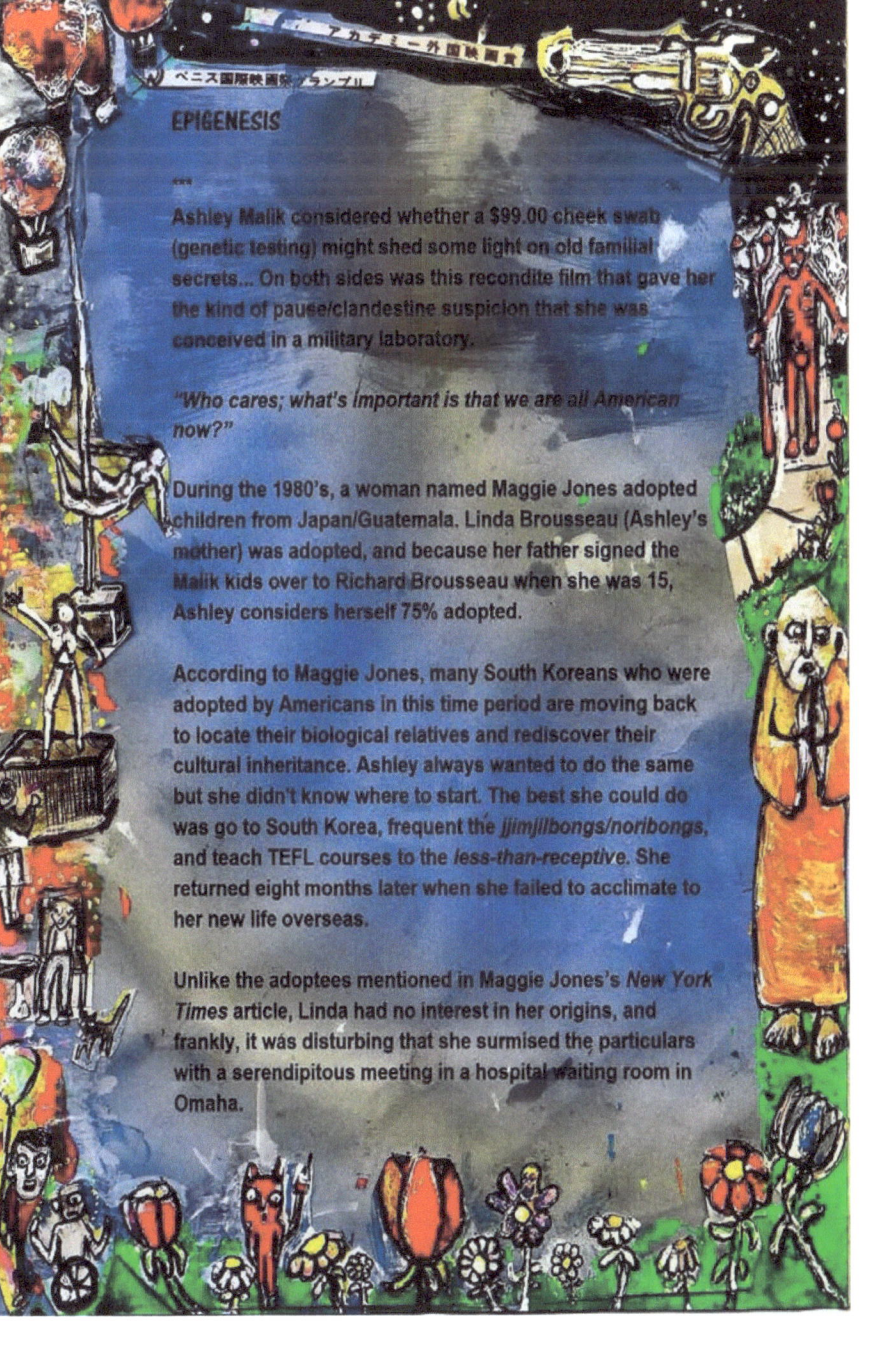

EPIGENESIS

***

Ashley Malik considered whether a $99.00 cheek swab (genetic testing) might shed some light on old familial secrets... On both sides was this recondite film that gave her the kind of pause/clandestine suspicion that she was conceived in a military laboratory.

"Who cares; what's important is that we are all American now?"

During the 1980's, a woman named Maggie Jones adopted children from Japan/Guatemala. Linda Brousseau (Ashley's mother) was adopted, and because her father signed the Malik kids over to Richard Brousseau when she was 15, Ashley considers herself 75% adopted.

According to Maggie Jones, many South Koreans who were adopted by Americans in this time period are moving back to locate their biological relatives and rediscover their cultural inheritance. Ashley always wanted to do the same but she didn't know where to start. The best she could do was go to South Korea, frequent the *jjimjilbongs/noribongs*, and teach TEFL courses to the *less-than-receptive*. She returned eight months later when she failed to acclimate to her new life overseas.

Unlike the adoptees mentioned in Maggie Jones's *New York Times* article, Linda had no interest in her origins, and frankly, it was disturbing that she surmised the particulars with a serendipitous meeting in a hospital waiting room in Omaha.

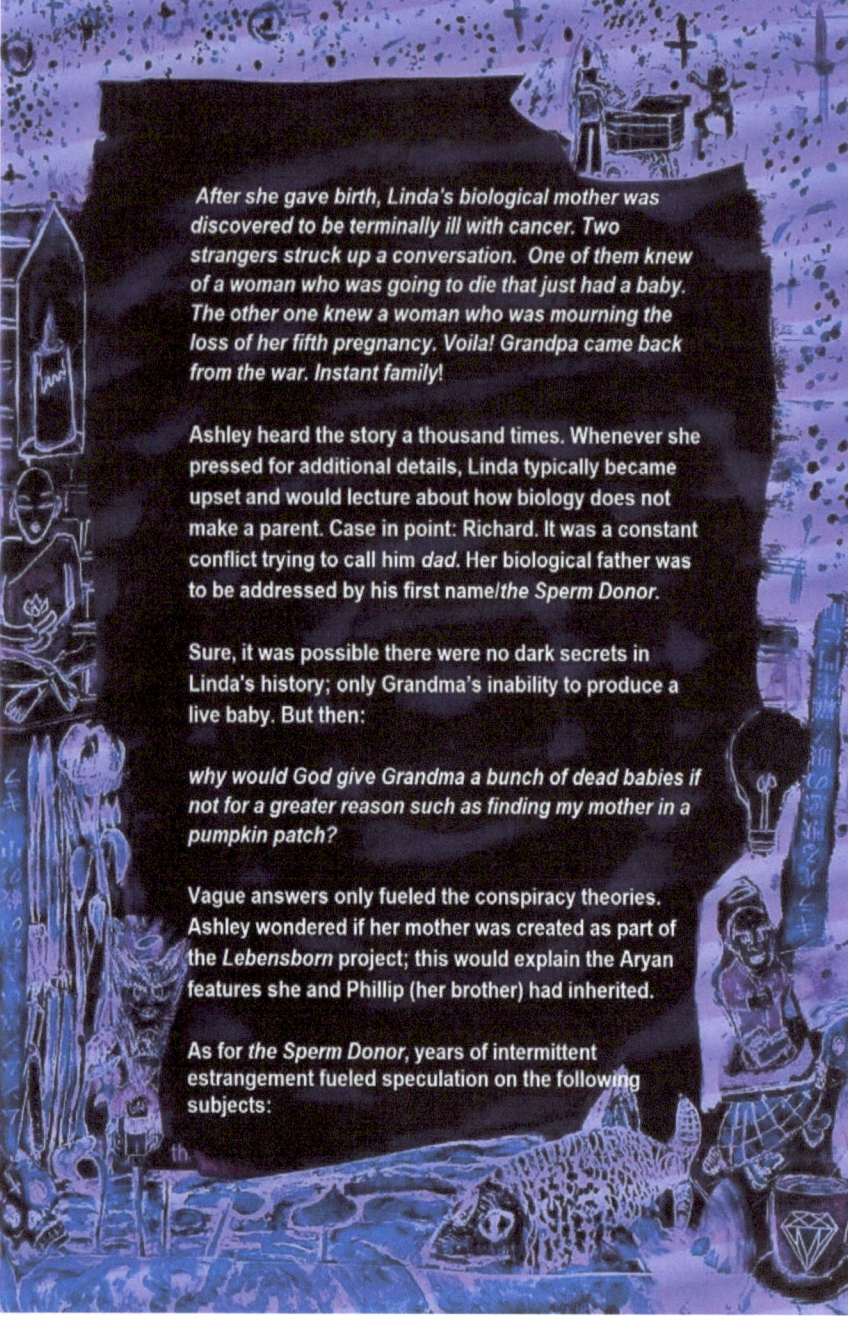

After she gave birth, Linda's biological mother was discovered to be terminally ill with cancer. Two strangers struck up a conversation. One of them knew of a woman who was going to die that just had a baby. The other one knew a woman who was mourning the loss of her fifth pregnancy. Voila! Grandpa came back from the war. Instant family!

Ashley heard the story a thousand times. Whenever she pressed for additional details, Linda typically became upset and would lecture about how biology does not make a parent. Case in point: Richard. It was a constant conflict trying to call him *dad*. Her biological father was to be addressed by his first name/*the Sperm Donor*.

Sure, it was possible there were no dark secrets in Linda's history; only Grandma's inability to produce a live baby. But then:

why would God give Grandma a bunch of dead babies if not for a greater reason such as finding my mother in a pumpkin patch?

Vague answers only fueled the conspiracy theories. Ashley wondered if her mother was created as part of the *Lebensborn* project; this would explain the Aryan features she and Phillip (her brother) had inherited.

As for *the Sperm Donor*, years of intermittent estrangement fueled speculation on the following subjects:

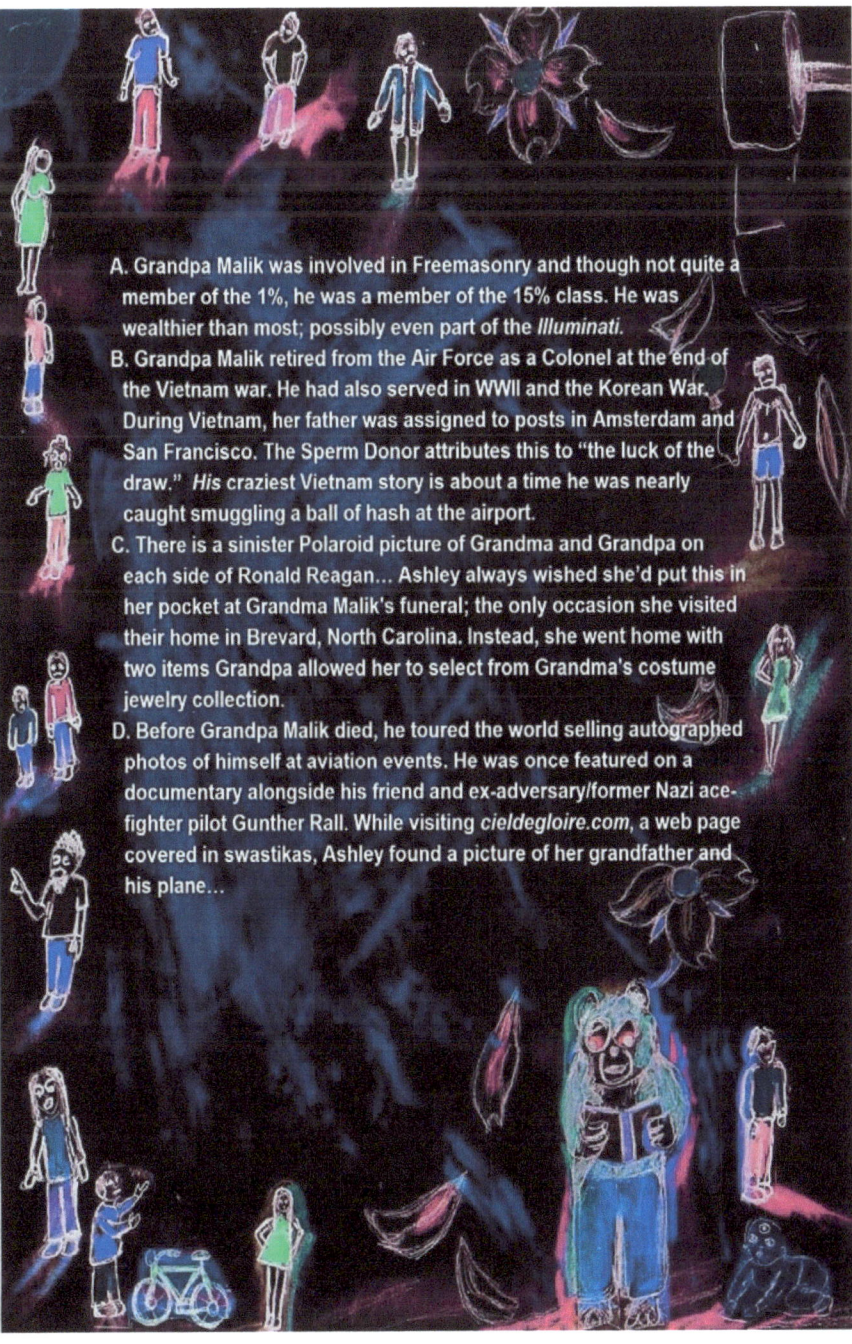

A. Grandpa Malik was involved in Freemasonry and though not quite a member of the 1%, he was a member of the 15% class. He was wealthier than most; possibly even part of the *Illuminati*.

B. Grandpa Malik retired from the Air Force as a Colonel at the end of the Vietnam war. He had also served in WWII and the Korean War. During Vietnam, her father was assigned to posts in Amsterdam and San Francisco. The Sperm Donor attributes this to "the luck of the draw." *His* craziest Vietnam story is about a time he was nearly caught smuggling a ball of hash at the airport.

C. There is a sinister Polaroid picture of Grandma and Grandpa on each side of Ronald Reagan... Ashley always wished she'd put this in her pocket at Grandma Malik's funeral; the only occasion she visited their home in Brevard, North Carolina. Instead, she went home with two items Grandpa allowed her to select from Grandma's costume jewelry collection.

D. Before Grandpa Malik died, he toured the world selling autographed photos of himself at aviation events. He was once featured on a documentary alongside his friend and ex-adversary/former Nazi ace-fighter pilot Gunther Rall. While visiting *cieldegloire.com*, a web page covered in swastikas, Ashley found a picture of her grandfather and his plane...

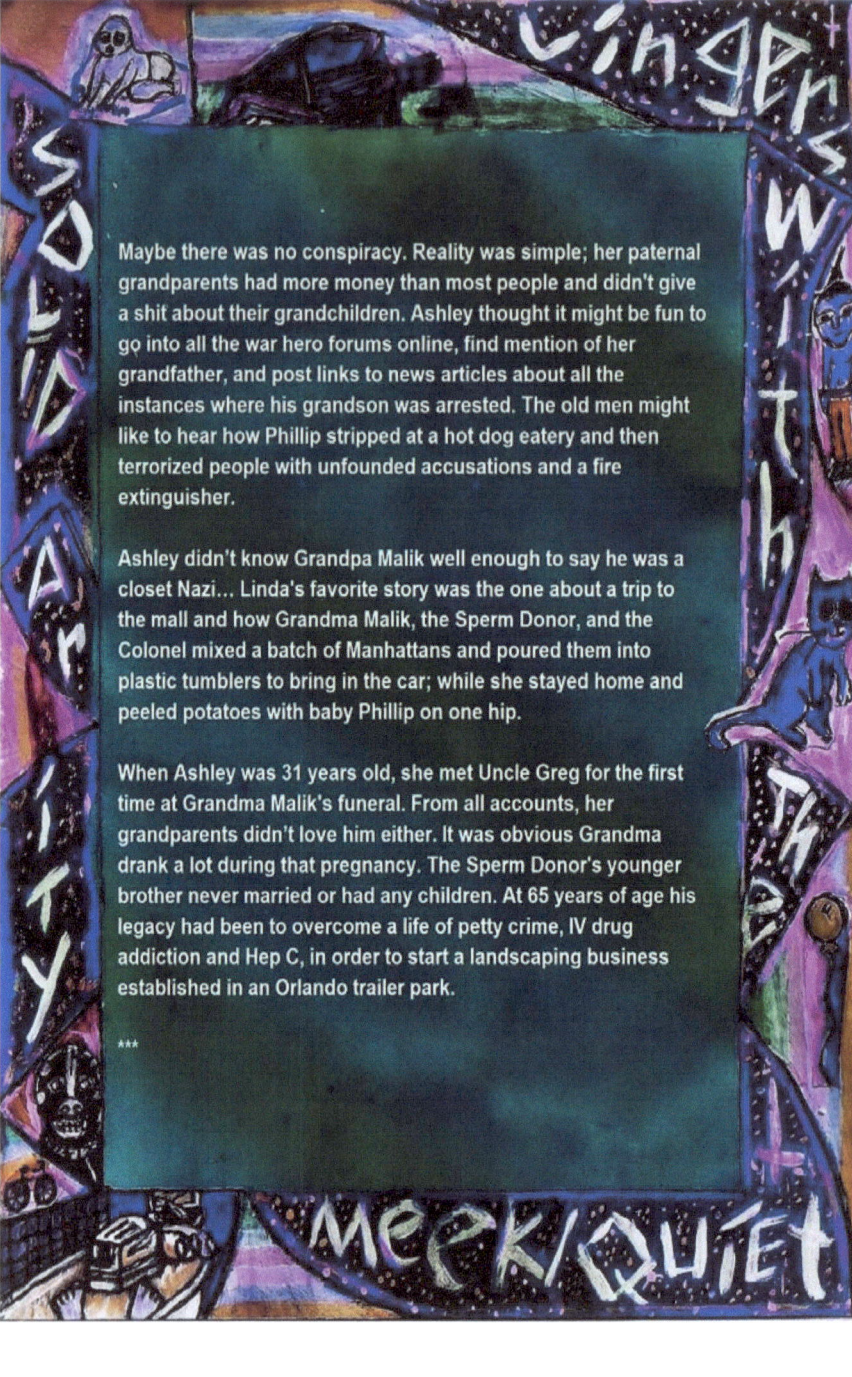

Maybe there was no conspiracy. Reality was simple; her paternal grandparents had more money than most people and didn't give a shit about their grandchildren. Ashley thought it might be fun to go into all the war hero forums online, find mention of her grandfather, and post links to news articles about all the instances where his grandson was arrested. The old men might like to hear how Phillip stripped at a hot dog eatery and then terrorized people with unfounded accusations and a fire extinguisher.

Ashley didn't know Grandpa Malik well enough to say he was a closet Nazi... Linda's favorite story was the one about a trip to the mall and how Grandma Malik, the Sperm Donor, and the Colonel mixed a batch of Manhattans and poured them into plastic tumblers to bring in the car; while she stayed home and peeled potatoes with baby Phillip on one hip.

When Ashley was 31 years old, she met Uncle Greg for the first time at Grandma Malik's funeral. From all accounts, her grandparents didn't love him either. It was obvious Grandma drank a lot during that pregnancy. The Sperm Donor's younger brother never married or had any children. At 65 years of age his legacy had been to overcome a life of petty crime, IV drug addiction and Hep C, in order to start a landscaping business established in an Orlando trailer park.

***

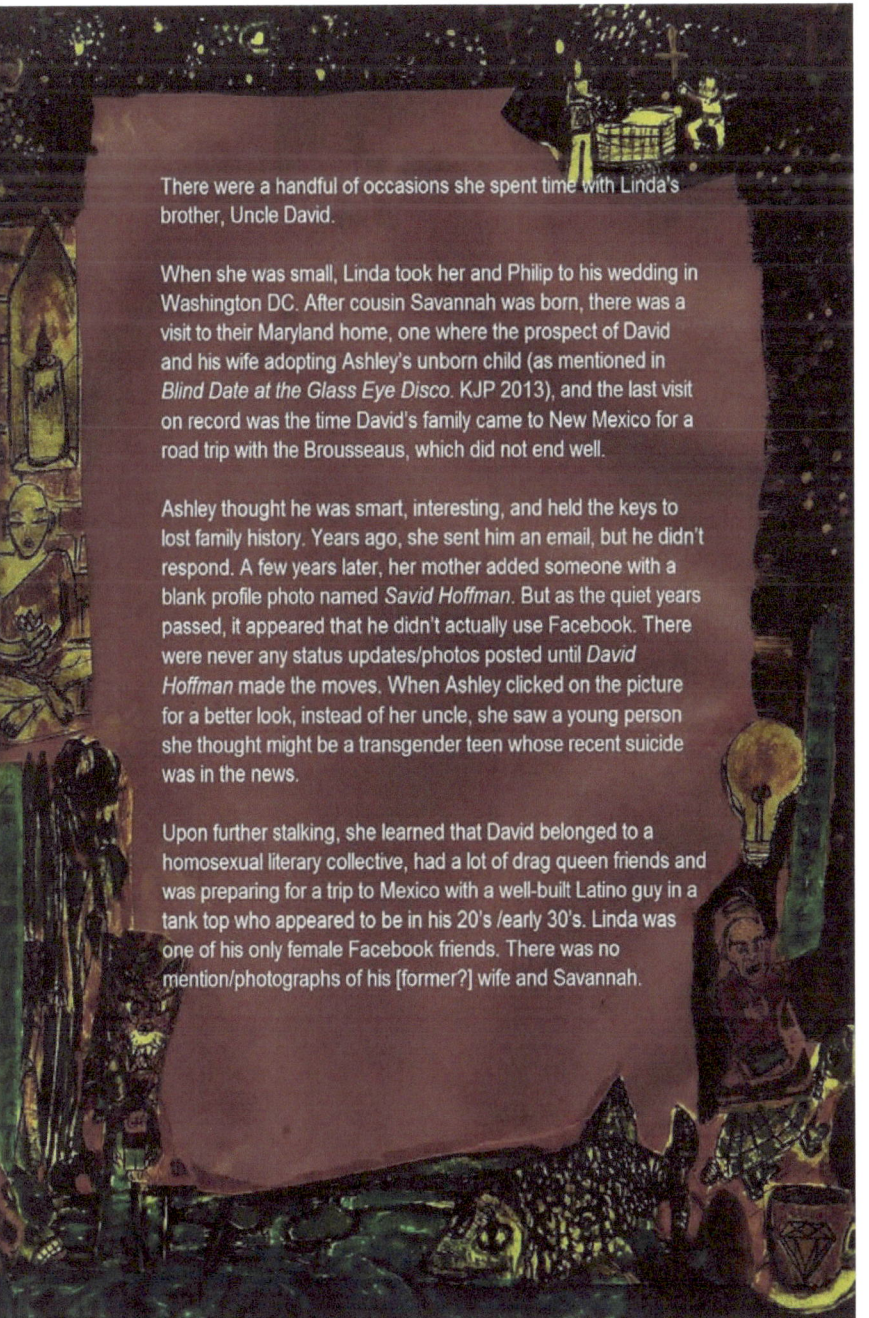

There were a handful of occasions she spent time with Linda's brother, Uncle David.

When she was small, Linda took her and Philip to his wedding in Washington DC. After cousin Savannah was born, there was a visit to their Maryland home, one where the prospect of David and his wife adopting Ashley's unborn child (as mentioned in *Blind Date at the Glass Eye Disco*. KJP 2013), and the last visit on record was the time David's family came to New Mexico for a road trip with the Brousseaus, which did not end well.

Ashley thought he was smart, interesting, and held the keys to lost family history. Years ago, she sent him an email, but he didn't respond. A few years later, her mother added someone with a blank profile photo named *Savid Hoffman*. But as the quiet years passed, it appeared that he didn't actually use Facebook. There were never any status updates/photos posted until *David Hoffman* made the moves. When Ashley clicked on the picture for a better look, instead of her uncle, she saw a young person she thought might be a transgender teen whose recent suicide was in the news.

Upon further stalking, she learned that David belonged to a homosexual literary collective, had a lot of drag queen friends and was preparing for a trip to Mexico with a well-built Latino guy in a tank top who appeared to be in his 20's /early 30's. Linda was one of his only female Facebook friends. There was no mention/photographs of his [former?] wife and Savannah.

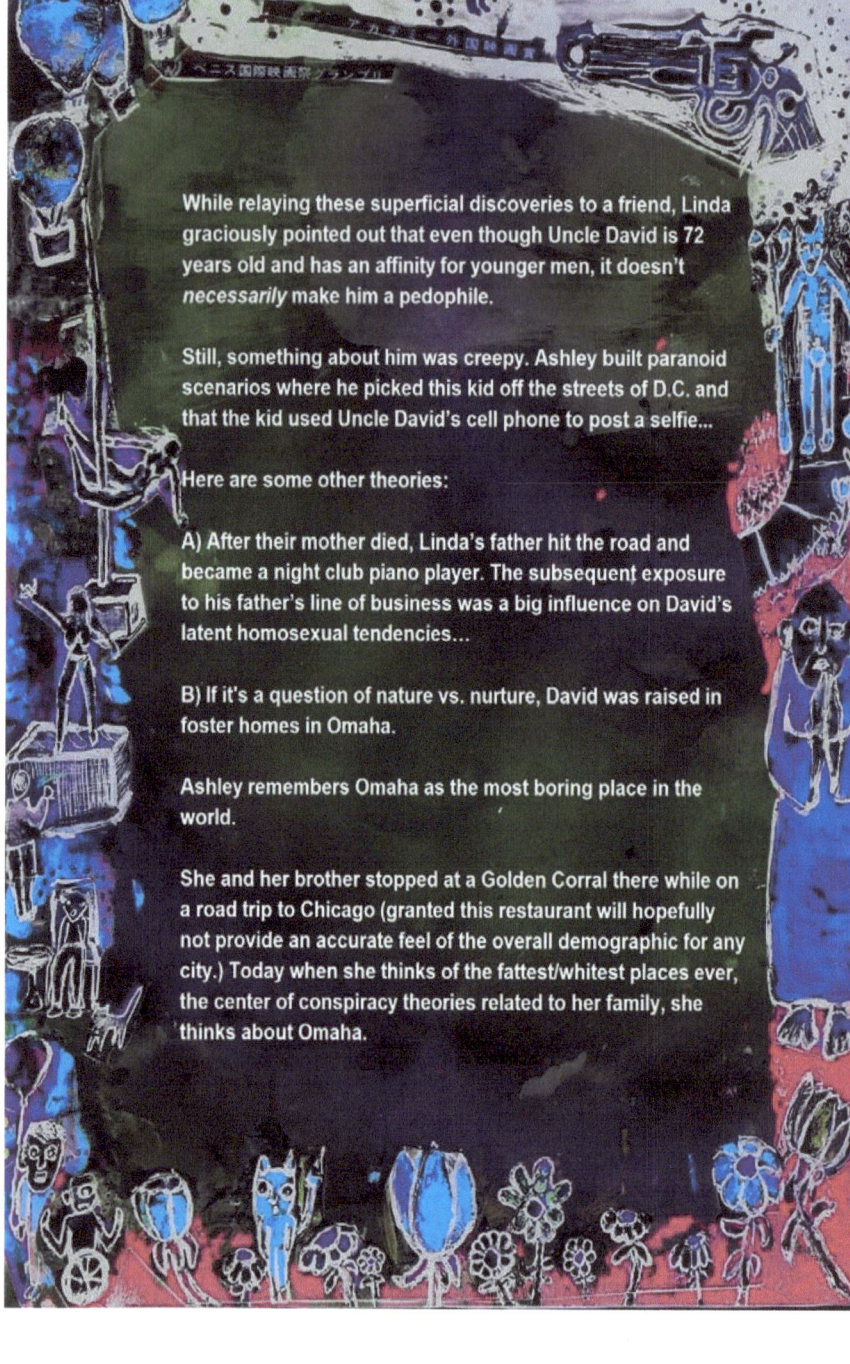

While relaying these superficial discoveries to a friend, Linda graciously pointed out that even though Uncle David is 72 years old and has an affinity for younger men, it doesn't *necessarily* make him a pedophile.

Still, something about him was creepy. Ashley built paranoid scenarios where he picked this kid off the streets of D.C. and that the kid used Uncle David's cell phone to post a selfie...

Here are some other theories:

A) After their mother died, Linda's father hit the road and became a night club piano player. The subsequent exposure to his father's line of business was a big influence on David's latent homosexual tendencies...

B) If it's a question of nature vs. nurture, David was raised in foster homes in Omaha.

Ashley remembers Omaha as the most boring place in the world.

She and her brother stopped at a Golden Corral there while on a road trip to Chicago (granted this restaurant will hopefully not provide an accurate feel of the overall demographic for any city.) Today when she thinks of the fattest/whitest places ever, the center of conspiracy theories related to her family, she thinks about Omaha.

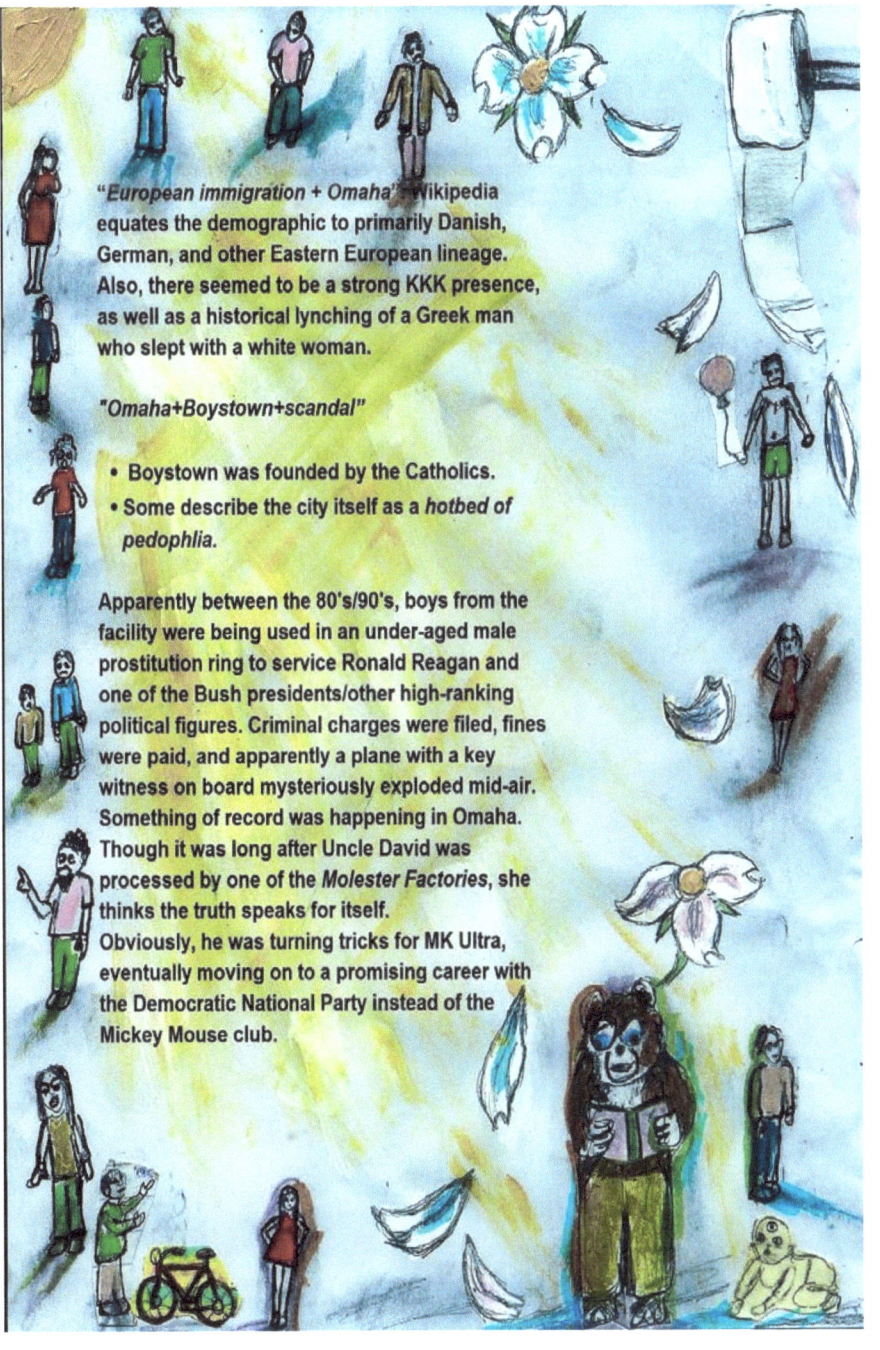

"*European immigration + Omaha*" Wikipedia equates the demographic to primarily Danish, German, and other Eastern European lineage. Also, there seemed to be a strong KKK presence, as well as a historical lynching of a Greek man who slept with a white woman.

"*Omaha+Boystown+scandal*"

- Boystown was founded by the Catholics.
- Some describe the city itself as a *hotbed of pedophlia*.

Apparently between the 80's/90's, boys from the facility were being used in an under-aged male prostitution ring to service Ronald Reagan and one of the Bush presidents/other high-ranking political figures. Criminal charges were filed, fines were paid, and apparently a plane with a key witness on board mysteriously exploded mid-air. Something of record was happening in Omaha. Though it was long after Uncle David was processed by one of the *Molester Factories*, she thinks the truth speaks for itself.
Obviously, he was turning tricks for MK Ultra, eventually moving on to a promising career with the Democratic National Party instead of the Mickey Mouse club.

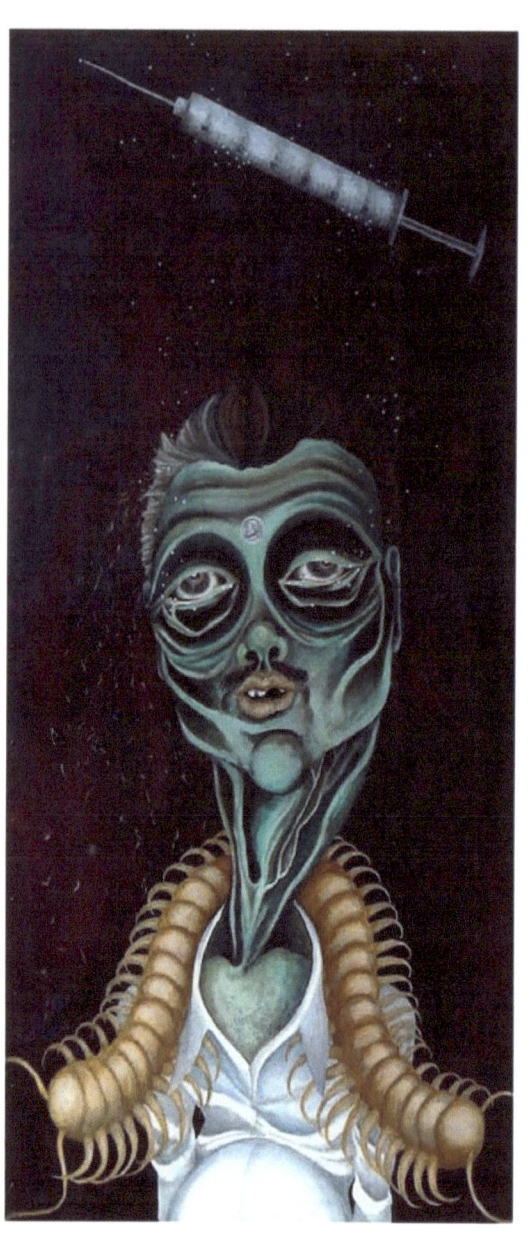

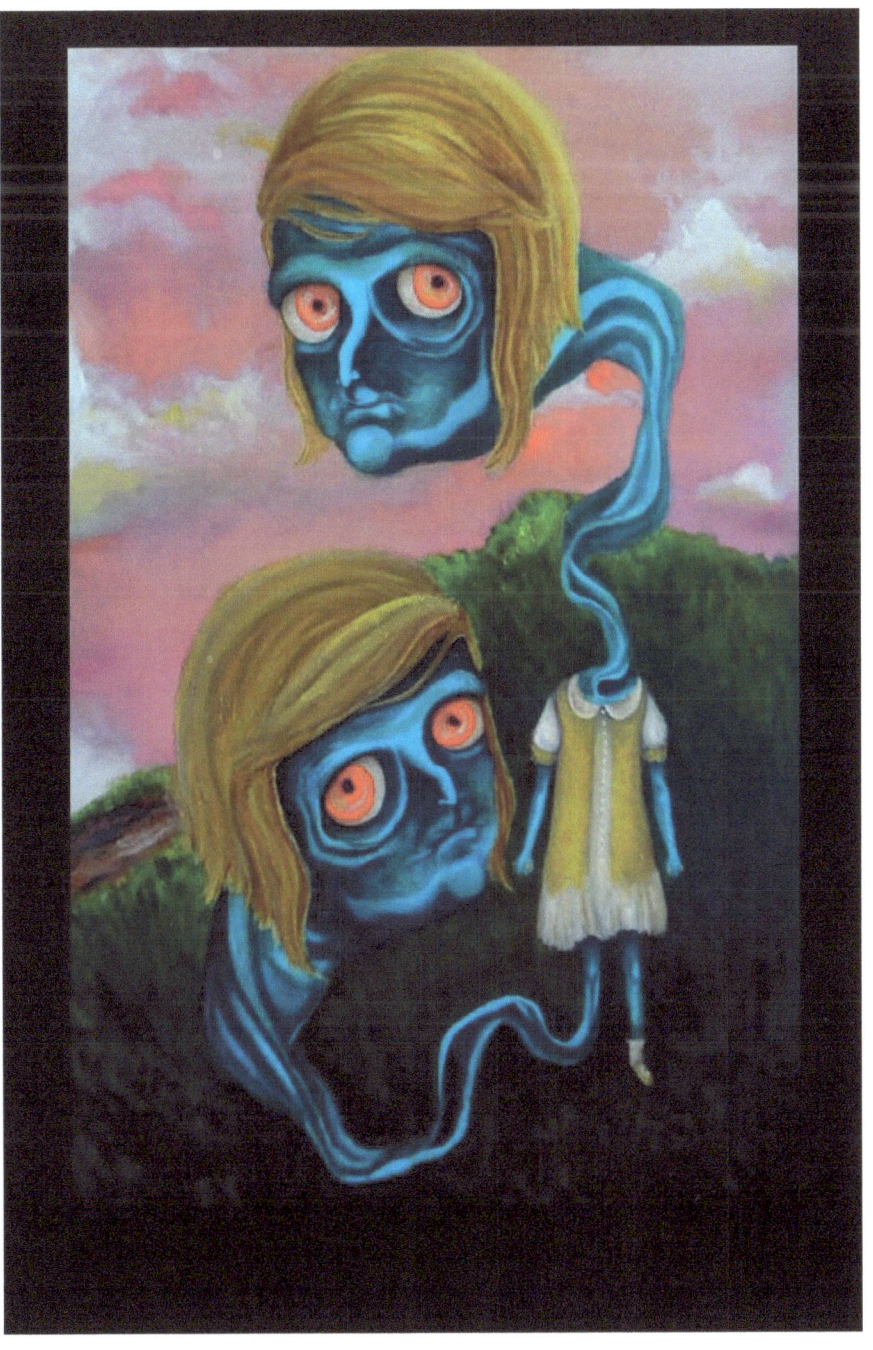

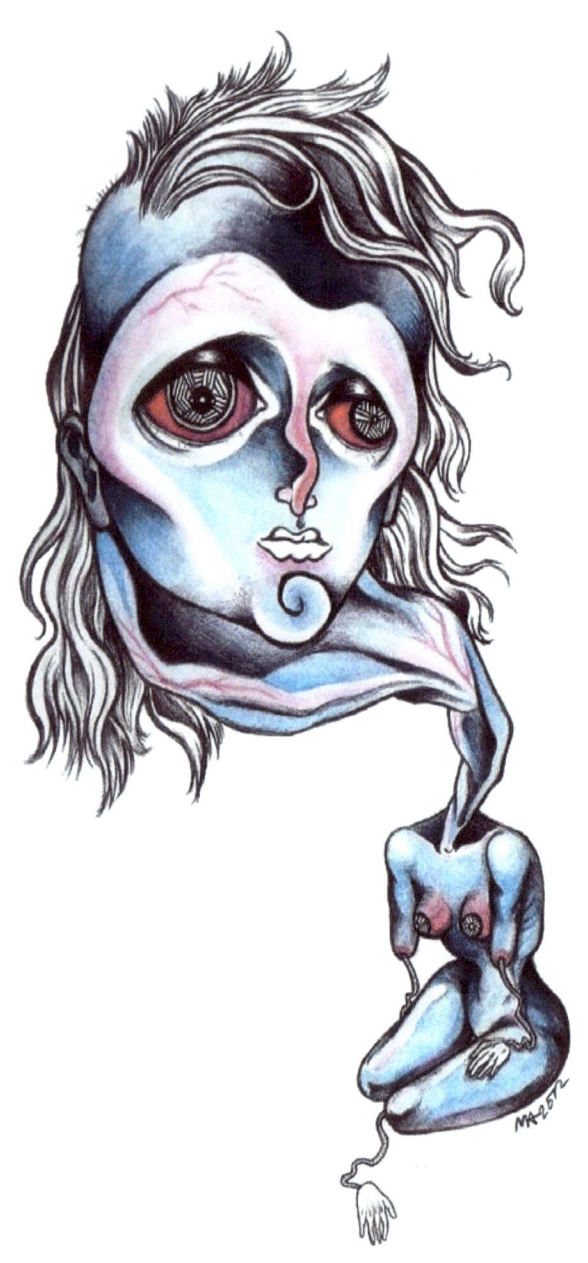

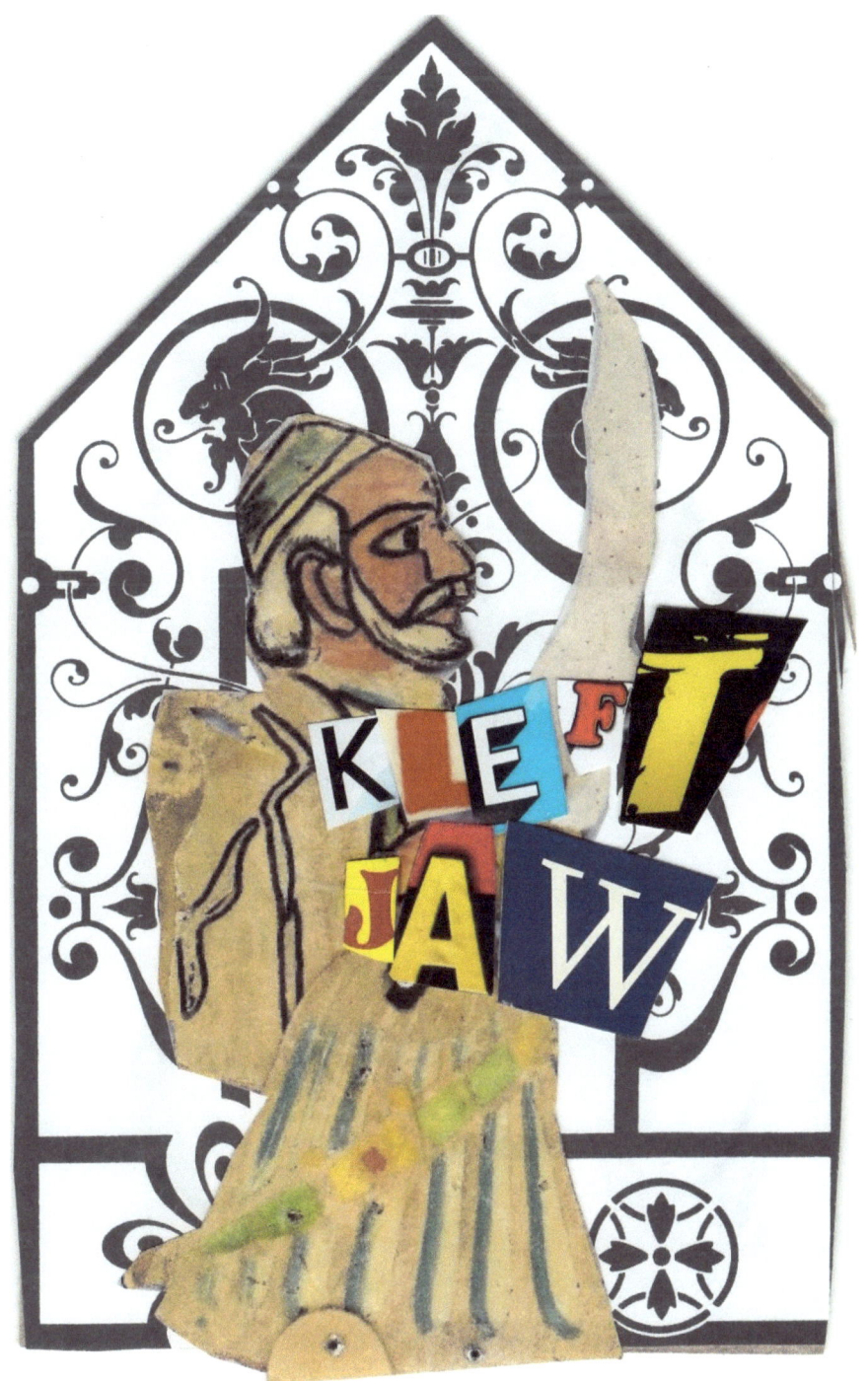